SANDOZ STUDIES, VOLUME 1

SANDOZ   *Series Editor*
STUDIES   Renée M. Laegreid

Founding Editor
John Wunder

SANDOZ STUDIES, VOLUME 1

Women in the
Writings of Mari Sandoz

Edited and with an introduction by
RENÉE M. LAEGREID and SHANNON D. SMITH

Foreword by JOHN WUNDER

University of Nebraska Press | Lincoln

Library of Congress
Cataloging-in-Publication Data
Names: Laegreid, Renee M., editor. |
Smith, Shannon D., 1958– editor.
Title: Women in the writings of
Mari Sandoz / edited and with an
introduction by Renee M. Laegreid and
Shannon D. Smith; foreword by John Wunder.
Description: Lincoln: University of Nebraska
Press, 2019. | Series: Sandoz studies; volume 1 |
Includes bibliographical references and index.
Identifiers: LCCN 2018048119
ISBN 9781496215956 (cloth: alk. paper)
ISBN 9781496216083 (epub)
ISBN 9781496216090 (mobi)
ISBN 9781496216106 (pdf)
Subjects: LCSH: Sandoz, Mari,
1896–1966—Criticism and
interpretation. | Women in literature.
Classification: LCC PS3537.A667 Z97 2019 |
DDC 813/.52—dc23 LC record available at
https://lccn.loc.gov/2018048119

Set in New Baskerville ITC Pro by E. Cuddy.
Designed by L. Auten.

Contents

Illustrations

Foreword

JOHN WUNDER

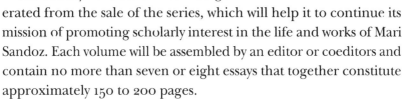

Welcome to the first volume of Sandoz
Studies, a series of thematically grouped
essays by Mari Sandoz or about Mari Sandoz and her work, published by the University of Nebraska Press in collaboration
with the Mari Sandoz Heritage Society.

The volumes of Sandoz Studies will be
published biennially. The series is created by the Mari Sandoz Heritage Society for its members, and with the hope
of expanding interest and research into
Mari Sandoz and her work to a broader
audience.

The society receives all revenue gen-
erated from the sale of the series, which will help it to continue its
mission of promoting scholarly interest in the life and works of Mari
Sandoz. Each volume will be assembled by an editor or coeditors and
contain no more than seven or eight essays that together constitute
approximately 150 to 200 pages.

The purpose of Sandoz Studies is threefold: (1) to make available
in published form a collection of essays either previously unpublished

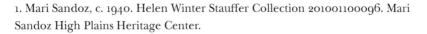

1. Mari Sandoz, c. 1940. Helen Winter Stauffer Collection 201001100096. Mari
Sandoz High Plains Heritage Center.

or published in dispersed publications and not easily accessible; (2) to provide new and existing society members with information and available scholarship on Sandoz and her writing; and (3) to provide a publication outlet for presentations from the annual meeting, student essays created in the Sandoz Writing Workshop, or other scholarly opportunities.

To administer Sandoz Studies, the Sandoz Society has created a three-person editorial board. Appointed by the society's president, the board oversees the choice of themes, volume editors, and production. One or two members of the editorial board act as peer reviewers of the volumes. Editorial board members serve jagged and renewable terms of five years each so that continuity would be ensured. Editorial board members may edit a volume, and if that is the case another board member will conduct the peer review of the volume. The first editorial board is composed of John Wunder (Lincoln, Nebraska), Renée Laegreid (Laramie, Wyoming), and Shannon Smith (Laramie, Wyoming). All three have won awards for their publishing activities. Laegreid and Smith have agreed to coedit the first volume on the women written about by Mari Sandoz. This editorial board will also be choosing future themes and volume editors.

This new series and its first volume are a labor of love and dedication by the editorial board and the Mari Sandoz Heritage Society. We hope that you enjoy it as much as we have enjoyed its preparation. Turn this page and discover ideas and new information about the works of Mari Sandoz.

Acknowledgments

The editors would like to thank *Great Plains Quarterly* for permission to reprint the essay by Glenda Riley.

Introduction

RENÉE M. LAEGREID AND
SHANNON D. SMITH

"Womens is everywhere!" Where that expression came from is unclear, but it is an appropriate introduction to Mari Sandoz and her writings on women. In the history and literature of the American West, women have been overshadowed by the actions and exploits of men; Native women and women of color even more so. Not so with Sandoz. From her first published story, "The Vine," onward, women have been a vital part of her work. The short writings and excerpt in this volume provide just a small sampling of Sandoz's skill at weaving women into the historical fabric of the Sandhills region. Importantly, her inclusion of women is not as an afterthought, not a form of contribution history, nor with a feminist agenda (despite the fact that Sandoz led a life that seemed to exemplify feminist ideals, she staunchly opposed early twentieth-century feminism). Instead, Sandoz wrote about the women she observed around her as integral players in the social, cultural, and political lives of their communities.

When Sandoz wrote about the women she knew and studied, she did not shy away from the sacrifices, hardships, and disappointments

2. Mari Sandoz in her Lincoln, Nebraska, apartment, 1939. Helen Winter Stauffer Collection 200300100068. Mari Sandoz High Plains Heritage Center.

they endured to forge a life in the harsh plains environment. But she also wrote about their moments of joy, friendships, and—for some—a connection to the land that encouraged them to carry on. While early scholarship on western women focused on white, middle-class women, from the beginning of her career, Sandoz's writings included Native American women, and women of all classes. Not always a literalist, Sandoz's descriptions of women in their plains environment move easily between the real and the metaphorical, as seen in the following selections. The scholarly essays that follow each of Sandoz's pieces help place her work into broader contexts, enriching our understanding of her as an author and as a woman deeply connected to the Sandhills of Nebraska.

RENÉE M. LAEGREID AND SHANNON D. SMITH

SANDOZ STUDIES, VOLUME 1

1

These Were the Sandhills Women

Stories, Images, and Mari Sandoz

RENÉE M. LAEGREID

This title is adapted from the Mari Sandoz book *These Were the Sioux,* an introduction to the lives and ways of a people she had come to know and admire. For readers whose conceptions of Native Americans were likely based on movies, television, or Wild West stories, her book gently educated them, as she had been, "to catch a glimpse . . . into the meaning of the customs and beliefs of [the Sioux], a little like the view from a high mountain as the mist begins to break over the far plains."[1] In this, as in other writings, she challenged the idea that all Native peoples could be lumped under one, monolithic heading: "Indian."

Sandoz's writings also challenged the idea that Sandhills women could be considered under equally reductive terms. Decades before scholars began to seriously challenge the frontier myth that emphasized a heroic, masculine experience, Mari Sandoz wrote of the diverse and complex women who called this region home. This essay will assess the women from Mari Sandoz's works, particularly

3. Mari Sandoz at the Lazy vv Ranch, Colorado, 1947. Special Collections, 080–02912, Love Library. University of Nebraska–Lincoln.

from *Old Jules, Miss Morissa,* and *Slogum House,* first by exploring stereotypes of frontier women, then by connecting women in Sandoz's stories to larger social and cultural influences, all the while showing how Mari Sandoz's women defied simple characterization.

When Euro-American settlers moved into the West, they brought with them more than material possessions; they carried along their beliefs about proper roles for men and women. John Mack Faragher writes of gender arrangements during the nineteenth century, generally agreeable to both sexes: "men enjoyed a monopoly on public life; the vast majority of women had to accept the position in the social order occupied by their husbands, fathers, or brothers. Women enjoyed a private social and cultural life which they created themselves, but it was of little consequence in the allocation of social responsibility and power."[2] In their role of supporting cast, it should come as no surprise that women seldom received a prominent place in literature or artistic depictions of the pioneer saga. "If women entered the landscape at all," Susan Armitage and Betsy Jameson note, "they were either brief diversions in a saloon or brothel, or they were hazy supporting figures far in the background, stoically oppressed or angelically supportive, and certainly voiceless and passive."[3] Simply put, women had limited storylines in the frontier story, appearing as either a good woman, a sad woman, or a bad woman, stereotypes initiated and perpetuated by writers and historians alike. A brief discussion on gender history will, hopefully, illuminate the roots of these frontier stereotypes.

In preindustrial societies men and women had their specific areas, or spheres, of responsibility, although metaphorically they were more akin to concentric rings than spheres. Women had primary care of the central rings with home in the center, expanding outward to the kitchen garden, poultry yard, and dairy production. Men held responsibility for the outer rings that included tending of the fields, livestock, and barnyards. The rings, however, could easily be crossed as needed since the success of the family economy depended on everyone's participation. For example, women commonly helped in the fields during harvest, and men took care of domestic chores during illness or childbearing.

Permeable lines of gendered work hardened with the shift from a predominantly agricultural society to one based on industry and the unprecedented economic and social changes that accompanied that shift. The rise of new industries encouraged rural workers to leave the countryside for jobs in rapidly growing urban centers; growth of the capitalist economy opened possibilities for men from outside elite families to increase their earning power and enter the new middle class. Entry into the middle class required, among other status markers, a husband to earn sufficient income so that his wife and children did not have to work outside the home. The emphasis on women at home, no longer part of the family economy, became an important factor in establishing impermeable gendered spheres that defined middle-class status; women inhabited the private sphere of home and men the public sphere of business and politics.[4]

The concept of separate spheres, then, is a modern one. For the most part, as the industrial era dawned, men and women supported the idea that society functioned best when men and women stayed in their respective and mutually beneficial spheres. For men, their responsibilities revolved around the unpleasant, competitive, and amoral work of business and politics. This left women free to focus their lives within the private sphere of the home, on domestic responsibilities, rearing children, and providing a moral foundation for the family. These ideas associated with separate spheres informed the social and cultural baggage that families packed and carried with them as they moved westward.[5]

One of the earliest depictions of pioneer women, and perhaps the most familiar, is of the good woman, the Madonna of the Prairie, the "gentle tamer" or "helpmate" of the westward-moving husband.[6] She embodied all the virtues of true womanhood: she was pious, pure, submissive, and domestic.[7] Her "commitment to family," writes historian Robert Griswold, "preceded and took precedence over a commitment to self." She was the self-sacrificing mother, the moral rock in the midst of a rushing and rapidly changing stream. The ideology of separate spheres, Griswold continues, "justified middle-class women's restricted, home-focused activities within a meaningful role in society, and by acknowledging women's position as moral guardians and civilizers within the home it allowed them to expand their influence outside the confines of the home." Middle-class women were considered natural advocates for all things related to their domestic sphere—culture, education, spiritual and intellectual ideas, health, and sanitation—not only in their own homes but as activists for reforms in their communities and beyond. Frontier women recognized the importance of their civilizing influence as their unique contribution to expanding America's empire.[8] The vast majority of frontier women, in the Sandhills, as elsewhere, fully embraced the concept of separate spheres and their role in it.

The second trope is the reluctant frontier wife, good women who accompanied their husbands westward, but not happily. The idea that "stoically oppressed" women suffered deeply from isolation and a harsh, unfamiliar pioneer environment became firmly entrenched in the public mind, and became a stock element in film and fiction. The 1929 silent film *The Wind* tells the story of a young socialite from civilized Virginia who moves to the uncivilized West. Slowly but surely, frontier conditions and the winds—the relentless winds—drove her insane.[9]

Historian Walter Prescott Webb uncritically accepted the frontier insanity myth and added the weight of scholarly authority to it. In *The Great Plains* (1931), Webb writes, "The Great Plains in the early period was strictly a man's country. . . . There was a zest to the life, adventure in the air, freedom from restraint." But apparently, the plains weren't so good for the women. "Most of the evidence," he reports, "reveals that the Plains repelled the women as they attracted the men. . . . The early conditions on the Plains precluded the little luxuries that women love and that are so necessary to them. . . . The wind alone drove some to the verge of insanity."[10]

4

While Webb did not invent the idea of the frontier driving women mad, he lent credibility to the myth in academic scholarship and in the popular imagination.

Within a few years after the publication of *The Great Plains*, Mari Sandoz's stories of the northern plains became available to readers. In her first book, *Old Jules* (1935), Sandoz does not shy away from the effects frontier life could have on settler women as she traces the mental decline of Henriette, the second of Jules's four wives. Shortly after Henriette divorced Jules, he began to worry about her; as Sandoz writes, "He believed she was going the way of so many women there during the dry years."[11] As the long years of drought continued, Henriette, like many others, suffered, and was finally "taken to the asylum."[12] While the history of the West is full of stories of crazy people, not all, or even most, were women. In Nebraska the first asylum opened in Lincoln in 1870, three years after statehood. High demand led to a second one in Norfolk in 1885 and a third in Hastings in 1891.[13] In her books and essays, Sandoz writes of the men as well as the women whose relatives put them on a train headed to an asylum.[14] Nineteenth-century census records support her observations: men and women went to asylums in fairly equal numbers.[15]

And then, of course, there are the bad women, the "brief diversions in a saloon or brothel," the "soiled doves," "fallen angels," "painted ladies of the night."[16] It was so easy to land in this category: balancing atop the "True Womanhood" pedestal was hard; with just a single misstep a woman could fall, irredeemable, from grace. One of the surest ways for a good girl to go wrong was to "go to the bushes"—one of Sandoz's favorite euphemisms—with her beau. This lapse of purity indicated failure on a number of levels. A woman who agreed to premarital sex indicated a personal failing, of course—she should have just said no. She failed the man, too. Had her moral character been sufficient, she would have convinced him of the inappropriateness of his desires. Not only did she fail herself and her beau, but also her family and her community; for her transgression she suffered banishment to the margins of society.

Sandoz doesn't take such a black-and-white view of the issue, and the story of Victoria and Ed, in *Old Jules*, serves as a fine example.[17] Fifteen-year-old Victoria and Ed, her older boyfriend, are in love. As sometimes happens, they go to the bushes, and she becomes pregnant. Before she tells Ed, Victoria's older sister, Maggie, arrives in town to visit her family. Victoria confides in her sister, who then seduces Ed, tells him she is pregnant, and although she knows she is not, threatens him into marrying her. When Victoria's condition becomes obvious she is shunned by the townspeople, especially the women. After her baby arrives Victoria leaves to find work in a new town, but she cannot escape her reputation. Once again, she finds herself ostracized. Alone, desperate, and certain she can never escape the humiliation of having a baby out of wedlock, Victoria takes her own life.[18] In the story of Ed and Victoria, Sandoz does not moralize. Instead, she allows readers to come to their own conclusions about the unforgiving moral standards and who the bad woman, or women, may be. Throughout her works, Sandoz effectively challenges rigid gender norms, as well as the assumption that women fit neatly within one-dimensional stereotypes. Her observations and experiences with Sandhills women refute easy labels, giving readers multifaceted characters whose personal histories intersect with the social and cultural climate of their times.

Mari Sandoz's first book, *Old Jules*, begins with his arrival in Chadron, Nebraska, in 1884. While this date aligns with the early years of Euro-American settlement in the region, it is rather late in terms of westward expansion. Euro-Americans began immigrating to Oregon Territory in the late 1830s, the Mormons began traversing the plains on their way to Utah in 1846, and yet another flood of immigrants ventured across the region after the United States took control of California and news of the gold strike at Sutter's Mill got out in 1849. Kathryne Lichty writes, "In the hundreds of journals and diaries of

         RENÉE M. LAEGREID

the pioneers on the Oregon and Mormon trails there is nothing to indicate that these land seekers even knew the Sandhills existed."[19] Even if they did, reports from explorers hardly made the Sandhills seem an inviting destination. From Zebulon Pike's description of "barren soil, parched and dried up for eight months of the year," to Stephen Long's assessment of it as "almost wholly unfit for cultivation, and of course uninhabitable for a people depending on agriculture for their subsistence," to topographical engineer G. K. Warren's opinion that the Sandhills were "exceedingly solitary, silent, and depressing to one's spirits," there seemed few reasons to venture north of the Platte River, and many, many more to keep heading west.[20]

This is not to say that no one discerned the potential of the Sandhills region. A few cattlemen noticed the good grasses on the Sandhills in the late 1850s, along with clear streams and ponds in the valleys. Despite laws against trespassing on Indian land, these early cattlemen began amassing herds, their encroachment into the region foreshadowing the rancher-settler wars that would become a recurring theme in Sandoz's writings. Farm settlement began in earnest during the early 1880s, only after Native American lands had been confiscated and the people confined to reservations. During the thirty or forty years between the first Euro-American immigrants who traversed the region and Sandhills settlements, important legal changes had occurred that affected women in terms of land rights, transportation, and opportunities for work outside the home.

When settlement began in the late 1870s, Sandhills women benefited from reforms in women's property rights that had occurred between 1838 and 1862. The first reform involved changes in marriage property laws to allow married women to own property in their own right. When overland migration began, American marriage laws still reflected their English common law heritage. Although adjustments to marriage laws fell under the jurisdiction of individual states, nationwide they were "based on the simple presumption that 'in the eyes of the law' the husband and wife were one person—the husband."[21] Once the ring was on her hand, the wife disappeared as a legal entity: the husband acquired all the personal property the wife possessed at the time of marriage—money, goods, debts owed her, even her clothing and personal affects. He "could conduct business with regard to the property, manage it, and use the rents and profits."[22] Should he make bad business decisions, creditors could seize what had been her property to pay his debts.

During the era of migration to Oregon Territory in the 1830s, flaws with this system became increasingly apparent. The economic Panic of 1837—America's first and, at the time, worst depression— left thousands of women and children homeless and destitute. In an effort to protect women, state legislatures began enacting property-law reforms. By the end of the 1840s, most states had constructed new laws that allowed wives to own property separately from their husbands, protected her property from his creditors, and, occasionally, granted wives the right to manage and control property. The next major reform would come from the federal government, which had lagged behind the states in property reform. Federal law did not allow women to buy public land or file on free land, nor had federal land acts "ever exempted married women's property from the claims of their husbands."[23]

Events related to Oregon Territory extended property rights to women at the federal level. As mentioned earlier, Americans had been moving into the territory since the 1830s, even though it had been jointly held with Great Britain since 1818.[24] In this nebulously governed area, American settlers adopted their own provisional government and laws for dealing with land claims. Settlers, married men, single men over eighteen, and widows, could record a claim for land. In 1846, after years of wrangling, the United States and Great Britain finally divvied up Oregon; the following year the American part became an official U.S. territory. The transition to federal oversight meant a reassessment of provincial law. After review, Congress allowed all laws from the provisional government to

RENÉE M. LAEGREID

remain in effect except those "making grants of land, or otherwise affecting or encumbering the title to lands."[25] Settlers considered this reappraisal a huge disappointment, especially since Congress offered no alternative for Oregon Territory settlers on how to dispense public lands. This created, in the words of a legal historian, "a significant vacuum."[26]

Nationally, debates on how best to distribute public lands had been going on for many years. As individual territories were added to the Union, territorial governments developed the strategy of petitioning Congress for "donations" of free lands to distribute. Congress especially liked to use these donations to entice settlement "in distant or dangerous territories."[27] When Oregon territorial representative Samuel R. Thurston introduced the Oregon Donation Act of 1850, Congress quickly passed it.[28] In some respects Thurston's bill was typical: "It permitted settlers on unsurveyed lands to select claims [of 320 acres] without regard to legal subdivisions."[29] In another sense, the bill was revolutionary, setting a new precedent by stipulating, "If married before December 1, 1851, a couple received an additional 320 acres in the wife's name. This is the first time a federal land act gave land grants to women in their own right."[30] As an aside, the act apparently worked like a love tonic. From passage of the act in September 1850 until the December 1 deadline in 1851, marriage rates reached unprecedented levels in Oregon Territory.[31]

The state reforms that allowed married women to own property and the federal reform that allowed married women access to public domain lands were important stepping stones to the Homestead Act. Passed in 1862, the Homestead Act stipulated that "any person who is the head of a family, or who has arrived at the age of twenty-one years, and is a citizen of the United States, or who shall have filed his declaration of intention to become such, as required by the naturalization laws of the United States, and who has never borne arms against the United States Government or given aid and comfort to its enemies" could enter a claim for 160 acres of available land in the public domain.[32] Women now had the unprecedented and extraordinary opportunity to stake a claim on land, prove it up, and keep the land in their name.

In the Sandhills region, Euro-American settlement began in earnest after passage of the Homestead Act. The majority of women who migrated to the Sandhills did indeed fall into the "good woman" category: married and willing to sacrifice familiar comforts to help her family establish a new life on the plains. Wearing dress, gloves, and the ubiquitous bonnet, these frontier women often worked side by side with their husbands, engaging in traditionally male chores to help establish their new homes. Married women not only helped build the family's farm or ranch with her labor, but they could also use the new Homestead Act to claim acreage. Not just wives contributed to the family land base; other female members of the family—mothers, spinster aunts, and daughters—also used the Homestead Act to increase family holdings by claiming land in their own right. If adjacent land was not available, then land nearby could serve just as well. Old Jules found "one of the finest quarters in the country" for his mother-in-law, "not so far that she couldn't go there a few nights a month to establish a residence."[33] Gulla Slogum, discussed in more detail later, used and abused land laws to amass a ranching empire for her family.

For settler women, the hard, physical work of establishing a new home was seen as a necessary, but temporary, expediency. The goal for frontier families was to resume the middle-class ideal of separate spheres as soon as possible, with the men and women of the family engaging in the familiar roles they left behind. Once the homestead had been established, women could then turn their full attention to domestic concerns and to their role as community builders. To Webb's assertion that isolated, crude, and austere pioneer conditions broke women's spirits, Andrea Radke-Moss argues, "The daunting distances from town centers drove most women, not to despair, but to seek creative adaptations to their environment. For themselves and their children they sought domestic and cultural refinement, agricultural improve-

RENÉE M. LAEGREID

ments through gardening and agricultural extension programs, primary and secondary education, improved economic developments, and expanded political participation."[34]

By giving women the legal right to own property in their own names, the Homestead Act also helped protect women, as earlier reform laws had intended. Estelle Chrisman Laughlin recalls the story of Joe and Rosanna Smith, homesteaders in the Sandhills:

> Rosanna had done the real labor of holding down the claim and establishing a residence. After 18 months spent there, with the necessary $1.25 per acre saved and in his wallet, Joe Smith, in company with [the land locator] Fairfield and some others had gone to the land office to make filing. Strong drink had a hold on Joe and before the filing was made, his fund sadly depleted, and in his befogged state of mind he made over a relinquishment to his companion. His wife, Rosanna, was aroused and contested this, with the result that she got the south 80 acres and Fairfield the north 80 acres.[35]

Laughlin makes no more mention of Joe, which perhaps is not surprising considering how poorly he handled the couple's land filing. The married women's property reforms helped Rosanna, as it did others, to maintain a home regardless of a husband's unfortunate business dealings.

Single women not associated with a family also homesteaded in the Sandhills. According to Sheryll Patterson-Black's pioneering essay, single women claimed from 5 to 20 percent of public domain land, depending on time and place.[36] Some arrived to claim their homesteads as a single woman, met a nice bachelor, and married. Others remained single by choice. Sandoz weaves stories of unmarried women, or women without husbands who defied standard convention, into her books. In *Slogum House*, the character Old Moll chose to live alone. Known around the county for her handsome white mules and for operating "the finest hauling outfit in the country," Old Moll kept to herself. She told neighbors she "kicked her past in the pants and came West," moved to the Sandhills, and never looked back. Nor did she ever reveal details of her mysterious past.[37]

Mari Sandoz based her novel *Miss Morissa* largely on the story of the Sandhills physician Georgia Arbuckle Fix, who moved into the region in the 1880s.[38] Dr. Fix serves as an example of American social transformations brought about by the Industrial Revolution during the post–Civil War era. The new modern, industrial economy created career opportunities for educated, unmarried, middle-class women.[39] "New Women," as they came to be called, chafed at traditional social and cultural barriers that limited their opportunities to the domestic sphere; they fought for women's legal rights and access to professional education and careers. Most commonly stereotyped as masculinized, urban suffragettes, in the 1880s, New Women began to make inroads into previously all-male professions. Georgia Arbuckle graduated from the Omaha Medical School in 1884, the only woman in her class of nine students. After graduation she began a practice in Omaha. Two years later she moved to the Sandhills.

In 1939 Estelle Chrisman Laughlin wrote a reminiscence of the doctor: "Her step-father . . . and half-brother . . . had completed a contract for building a mile of road bed for the U.P. near Callaway, Nebraska, some time before. They brought tales of the free, open frontier to the young woman doctor in Omaha. Looking over the various fields open to the medical profession, the new west attracted her."[40] In *Miss Morissa*, Sandoz adjusts the story somewhat, writing that the young doctor headed to the Sandhills to escape a broken heart—her engagement to a man from a well-to-do and highly respected family broken off when his sister discovers the doctor had been born out of wedlock and spent her childhood on a poor farm. It is unclear which version of the story is true, but Sandoz's version certainly makes a better plot device. Nevertheless, the era of New Women began the long process of opening opportunities for women outside the home. For some, like Dr. Arbuckle Fix, attending a professional school allowed her to fashion her own destiny, with or without a husband, a story that shares a certain symmetry with

RENÉE M. LAEGREID

Sandoz's own life. Arbuckle married after arriving in the Sandhills, divorced her husband when the relationship faltered, and with legal control over her property, continued her successful career as an unmarried woman physician.[41]

While family groups made up the majority of Sandhills settlers, unmarried women like Georgia Arbuckle represented one important type of settler group. Unmarried men formed another category, also important to Sandoz's stories of Sandhills women. Some bachelors moved to the Sandhills, hoping to entice a sweetheart back home to follow after establishing a homestead; others hoped to somehow meet a woman on the frontier who would marry him.

Glenda Riley writes that the enthusiasm for frontier marriage was common, noting that "homesteaders believed that married men made better farmers," and there is truth to that.[42] A wife would take care of the domestic responsibilities: prepare and preserve foods, tend the garden, make and take care of children, and of course, provide companionship. Her presence would free him to concentrate on building up the farm, tend the cattle if they had any, and many other responsibilities.

Aside from bachelors, the high mortality rates associated with childbirth often left a husband widowed and with children. Estelle Laughlin recalled one of Dr. Arbuckle Fix's tragic, yet not uncommon calls. In her biography, Laughlin writes that the doctor received

an urgent request . . . to hasten at once to a neighbor woman's bedside as she was losing strength rapidly. The doctor threw on a coat, grabbed her medicine kit, and with the team already hitched to the buggy started out across country for the little home where a brave woman was desperately fighting, not only for her own life but that of another as well. The doctor loosened the lines, and with encouraging words urged her ponies forward while Harward, riding beside them, lashed them with a buggy whip on a run, all the way. But with all that horses and humans could do, they arrived too late. Death had won the race.[43]

To a father with small children, losing a wife and mother posed enormous challenges in taking care of both home and farm.

The reality of widowhood is made visible in a photo of George Barnes, "a poor settler who lost his wife (in 1886), having three small children to take care of."[44] Barnes hired Sandhills photographer Solomon Butcher to take his portrait. In what might be called the frontier soddy genre, Butcher's images depict not only family members and the homestead, but also a catalogue of the family's prized possessions, running the gamut from canned goods to ox teams. The Barnes photo adheres to the genre, but with some telling differences. Barnes stands with his two young sons and daughter in front of their sod home, three horses and a wagon are displayed near the house. No mother or female relatives are in sight, nor are any of the domestic items commonly taken from the sod home and displayed out of doors for a photograph. Having to take care of both domestic and field work distracted Barnes from both: the two boys have outgrown their coats and pants, the cuffs or hems yet to be let down, and "heavy rains caused the roof of the sod house to collapse the morning the photograph was taken," a sign that weakness in the support beam had been overlooked.[45]

And so bachelors and widowers searched for wives. Some found local women. In *Old Jules*, Sandoz writes, "Perhaps the year had been good and the roads open to travel late, most of Jules's cronies were getting married. Even Big Andrew came to tell [Jules] of a widow woman who would have him. Ah, this, too, was like the free land and his friend Jules—unbelievable."[46] For those who needed to look further afield, trains and the postal service were a godsend. Trains delivered mail with more speed and efficiency than the Oregon settlers could have imagined. Letters went back and forth between hopeful settlers and their sweethearts. Friends and family wrote on behalf of bachelors, talking up their character and prospects to help find women willing to marry him, sight unseen. And surprisingly often it worked. Old Jules "pounded the calloused backs of his team" to the train station in Rushville to fetch not one, not two,

RENÉE M. LAEGREID

but three wives of his four wives that his family had campaigned on his behalf to marry him.[47]

A fair question to ask is why an unmarried woman would travel alone via train (or if traveling from the old country on steamships and trains) to marry a man she did not know, in a place she had never seen, and so far away from family and friends. Several factors help explain their motives. First, as noted, was the emphasis on marriage as a woman's proper role; secondly, few career opportunities existed that would allow single women to support themselves; and third, there were a lot of single men in the West and a lot of single women in the East. Julie Checkoway writes that in the United States there were "300,000 single women back east, a number augmented by Civil War widows." Women without marriage prospects weighed their options: marriage, or spinsterhood eking out a living giving lessons or taking in sewing, or prostitution. The more adventurous ones opted for a "chance for greater social and economic freedom away from home," and moved west.[48]

Personal letters from friends beckoned women into matrimony on the frontier. Newspapers played an important role as well, as "from Nebraska to Kansas and Wyoming . . . [newspapers] began to serve as forums for matchmaking, running regular 'matrimonial columns' of paid advertisements, frequently with accompanying photographs."[49] In an example of buyer beware, "Mari Sandoz recalled that her neighbors obtained many items, including wives, through catalogues." According to Sandoz, such advertisements described "the offerings rather fully but with, perhaps, a little less honesty than Montgomery Ward or Sears Roebuck."[50]

When Old Jules set out to find a new wife, he sought one from the middle class, like himself, one who fulfilled the expectations of middle-class womanhood. She should, of course, be pure, although Old Jules did not seem overly concerned with a potential wife's piety. He expected a wife to cook, clean, manage the home, tend the garden, and bear his children. And although Jules expected—demanded—submission, Sandoz depicts his wives as fully dimensional people who had minds of their own. Marriage to his first wife, Estelle, did not last long. "When [she], refused to build the morning fires," Sandoz writes, "to run through the frosty grass to catch up his team, Jules closed her mouth with the flat of his long, muscular hand, dumped their supply of flour and sugar to the old sow and pigs, and loaded up his belongings upon the wagon to leave her and Knox County behind him forever."[51] And so he did.

For his next three wives, Jules enlisted the help of friends and family to find suitable mates and to write letters on his behalf. Jules's sister Elvina convinced her friend and classmate from Switzerland, Henriette, to leave an elegant nanny position in Boston, travel to Rushville, Nebraska, and marry Jules. He picked her up at the Rushville station, much to the amusement of his friends. "Well, I be hung for a horse thief! You oughter see the woman Old Jules has wrangled himself," Jed Brown remarked to Big Andrews. "Got a few hundred dollars of her own, Jules was telling me, and he shore needs that!"[52] Jules fully expected Henriette to follow tradition and hand her money over to him. But Henriette, as Sandoz notes, "was determined upon disobedience," leading to a contest of wills that lasted their entire marriage.[53] In one example, Sandoz writes, "With his wife's money Jules wanted to build, like the peasants he saw in France, a granary, a horse stable, a chicken coop, and a pigpen, in a succession of lean-tos against the living quarters. Henriette waited until he was away on a hunt. Then she hired two men to build a story-and-a-half house, and laid out a yard with outbuildings." She also bought herself a wagon and team of horses, heading to town or to visit neighbors to escape isolation or Jules. Henriette endured five years with Jules before divorcing him, by the end of their tumultuous, often violent marriage, "giving as good as she got."[54] His third wife, Emilia, had been swayed by Jules's sister to move from Switzerland to the Niobrara. Although Emilia lacked Henriette's fighting spirit, within two weeks she had found an ally and orchestrated her escape.[55]

RENÉE M. LAEGREID

Jules's fourth and final wife, Mary, also traveled to the Sandhills, persuaded by a letter campaign. As with the others, Mary took care of Jules, the house, the yard, and whatever else he demanded of her. Ambivalent at first about staying with Jules, she weighed the beauty of the land and the possibilities of a good life with Jules against what life she might expect if she left. Once she became pregnant, she knew she had to stay. Sandoz writes of the abuses Mary endured, the disappointments and resentments that continued to build within her. But she also writes of strategies Mary devised to make the best of her life with Jules, and the ties with family and friends that helped her through the difficult years. After her first long, cold winter in the house, when the thaw finally came, and "grey April wept her dripping days away in mists that beaded every bush and tree," Mary took comfort knowing that "soon her mother and sister would be with her, her own people, with news from the Old Country."[56] Unlike Henriette and Emilia, Mary had given Jules all her money. And she had his children. If she left him, what would she do? How could she have supported herself and her children? She would have known the options, and they weren't good. Like so many of Sandoz's women, Mary struggled to make the best of her situation, finding strength if not solace, in herself, her family and friends, and the land around her.

Just as Sandoz encouraged readers to look beyond the stereotypes of good women, she also introduced readers to the varieties of bad women. Sandoz tells the story of Virginia and Ed with compassion and sympathy for the girl and her lover. In a very matter-of-fact style, Sandoz reminds readers that humans have their frailties, and that in the case of an out-of-wedlock pregnancy, the woman suffers from social censure far more than the man. In another example, the Bannel family, bad luck encouraged otherwise good people to go wrong. "Three crop failures were enough for the Bannels, living beyond the John Place," Sandoz wrote in *Old Jules*. "They laid out a race track in the dead grass, built on a room apiece for the three girls, and made money enough for red plush furniture with fringe."[57]

The family didn't start out with the intention of getting into the business of betting and brothels. Drought and crop failure led them to take that low road; although perhaps suggesting character flaws that allowed the family to take that low road so readily.

And then there is the truly wicked woman, the one whose intentions are malicious and evil from the very beginning. Regula Haber, or Gulla, made her character debut as a Roadhouse Schwartze in *Old Jules*, but is fully developed in *Slogum House*.[58] Gulla came from a violent, thieving, and dangerous family, living in a shack in an Ohio river bottom. She found work washing linens for the wealthy Slogum family, where she met the young Ruedy Slogum. Seeing her chance to move up the social ladder, Gulla lured Ruedy "into the bushes"; then claiming to be pregnant with his child, she trapped him into marriage. Instead of being welcomed into his family, as she planned, Ruedy's family disowned him for marrying so far beneath the family's station. With vengeance as her guide, Gulla moves Ruedy and their children west, to the Sandhills, devoting the rest of her long life to using all means, mostly illegal, to acquire land, wealth, and the status markers of high society. Her goal is to go back to Ohio and throw Ruedy's family's scorn for her back into their faces. But the trappings of middle-class status she acquires, the impression of a refined matriarch and of a good family she tries to construct, the atmosphere of gentility she enforces on her family, cannot hide her true nature. The image Sandoz depicts of Gulla's physical self are as grotesque and vile as Gulla's actions.

Part of what makes *Slogum House* such a disturbing story is that Sandoz inverts stereotypes. Gulla is an evil woman—the mirror opposite of the Madonna of the Prairie. Her husband, Ruedy, is not a strong family leader, but weak and ineffectual. She rears two of her daughters, the twins, to be high-class call girls, and two of her sons to be thieves, thugs, and killers. When Libby, the good daughter, tries to leave home, Gulla accuses her of being ungrateful—think of all that, she, the mother, had done for the family! To which Libby replies, "Do you think I don't know there must be people in the

RENÉE M. LAEGREID

world who manage to eat without lying, cheating, stealing, even murder and the prostitution of their daughters?"[59] Finding sympathy for truly bad characters like Gulla is not easy. Yet Sandoz has a way of challenging what makes "good" people "bad," to consider the influences of nature and nurture on an individual, the role of class in helping or hindering social mobility, social expectations, and cultural changes, all of which come together to develop good or bad characters. Readers are encouraged to question: What is good? What is bad? And by whose standards?

One aspect of the frontier era that continues to fascinate is the idea that settlers had the freedom to live a premodern life. Some settlers did move to the Sandhills to escape modernity and "the rise of an industrial establishment and the mass production of consumer goods, technological improvements in transportation and communication, the growth of cities, and an increasing flow of immigrants from Europe."[60] Others, however, moved to the Sandhills with the hope of building wealth from the land and natural resources, to have a chance at a bigger piece of the modern consumer pie. No matter their motivations, though, settlers could not or would not escape the social and cultural ideas they left behind. Ideas that shaped the proper roles for men and women shaped their views on categorizing how women should live, what defined a good woman, or a bad one. Magazines, novels, and even historians perpetuated these views until they became stale stereotypes.

Long before the women's movement began in the 1970s, or the study of western women's history emerged in the 1980s, Mari Sandoz wrote about the lives of her family, friends, and neighbors. She knew the women and wrote about them with remarkable clarity and honestly. She provided no simple definition for a good woman or bad woman. In her stories she shows us that stereotypes do not apply to Sandhills women. Mary and Henriette and Georgia and Libby and all the others—these were the Sandhills women—individuals, diverse and complex, creating lives for themselves and their families in the Sandhills of Nebraska.

I would like to thank the Mari Sandoz Heritage Society for the opportunity to present this lecture. Mari Sandoz Heritage Center 2015 Annual Pilster Lecture, September 17, 2015, Chadron, Nebraska.

1. Sandoz, *There Were the Sioux*, 10.
2. Faragher, *Women and Men on the Overland Trail*, 2.
3. Jameson and Armitage, editors' introduction to *Writing the Range*, 3.
4. See, for example, Cott, *Grounding of Modern Feminism*, and Welter, "Cult of True Womanhood," 151–74.
5. See Caughfield, *True Women and the Western Experience*; Kaplin, "Manifest Domesticity"; Jackson, *Domesticating the West*.
6. Stoeltje, "'A Helpmate for Man Indeed.'"
7. See especially Kaplin, "Manifest Domesticity," and Riley, *Female Frontier*.
8. Radke-Moss, "'Willing Challengers,'"49.
9. Jameson and Armitage, editors' introduction to *Writing the Range*, 3.
10. Webb, *Great Plains*, 505–6.
11. Sandoz, *Old Jules*.
12. Sandoz, *Old Jules*, 215.
13. "Hastings State Hospital," accessed September 6, 2015, http://www.rootsweb .ancestry.com/~asylums/hastings_nb/index.html. In the Hastings asylum in December 1916, there were 1,152 inmates: 405 women and 747 men.
14. Sandoz, *Old Jules*, 110.
15. N. B. Johnson, "Mad Pioneer Women," 392.
16. Jameson and Armitage, editor's introduction to *Writing the Range*, 3.
17. Sandoz, *Old Jules*, 261.
18. Sandoz, *Old Jules*, 286.
19. Lichty, "History of the Settlement of the Nebraska Sandhills," 20.
20. Lichty, "History of the Settlement of the Nebraska Sandhills," 15, 16, 19.
21. Norma Basch, "Invisible Women,"347.
22. Zeigler, "Uniformity and Conformity,"474–76.
23. Margaret Riddle, "Donation Land Claim Act, Spur to American Settlement of Oregon Territory, Takes Effect on September 27, 1850," http:// www.historylink.org/index.cfm?DisplayPage=output.cfm&file_id=9501 ,September6, 2015.
24. The U.S. and Britain jointly occupied Oregon Territory from 1818 until 1846, when the two countries settled on the 49th parallel as a boundary.

RENÉE M. LAEGREID

Polk campaigned on "Fifty-four forty or fight!" but once elected as president quite happily settled on the 49th parallel.

25. Chused, "Oregon Donation Act of 1850,"59. See also Chused, "Late Nineteenth Century Married Women's Property Law."

26. Chused, "Oregon Donation Act of 1850," 59.

27. Chused, "Oregon Donation Act of 1850," 54.

28. Chused, "Oregon Donation Act of 1850," 44.

29. "The Donation Land Claim Act of 1850 Law & Legal Definition," September 6, 2015, http://definitions.uslegal.com/t/the-donation-land-claim-act-of-1850/.

30. Chused, "Oregon Donation Act of 1850," 61.

31. Margaret Riddle, "Donation Land Claim Act," September 6, 2015, http://www.historylink.org/index.cfm?DisplayPage=output.cfm&file_id=950.

32. "Transcript of the Homestead Act (1862): http://www.ourdocuments.gov/doc.php?doc=31&page=transcript.

33. Sandoz, *Old Jules*, 218.

34. Radke-Moss, "'Willing Challengers,'" 49.

35. Laughlin, "Dr. Georgia Arbuckle Fix: Pioneer," 23, 24.

36. Patterson-Black, "Women Homesteaders on the Great Plains Frontier," 68. See also Lindgren, *Land in her Own Name*.

37. Sandoz, *Slogum House*, 14, 15.

38. Sandoz, *Miss Morissa*.

39. Zunz, *Making America Corporate*.

40. Laughlin, "Dr. Georgia Arbuckle Fix: Pioneer," 23.

41. Laughlin, "Dr. Georgia Arbuckle Fix: Pioneer," 27.

42. Riley, *Building and Breaking Families in the American West*, 14.

43. Laughlin, "Dr. Georgia Arbuckle Fix: Pioneer," 25.

44. "Three motherless children and a caved in soddy," George Barnes family, photo by Solomon Butcher, American Memory (Library of Congress), *Prairie Settlement: Nebraska Photographs and Family Letters, 1862–1912*, http://memory.loc.gov/cgi-bin/query/h?ammem/psbib:@field%28docid+@lit%28p10002%29%29; http://www.nebraskastudies.org/0500/frameset_reset.html?http://www.nebraskastudies.org/0500/stories/0501_0112.html; and especially http://www.eyewitnesstohistory.com/photofrm3.htm.

45. "Three motherless children and a caved in soddy," George Barnes family, photo by Solomon Butcher, American Memory (Library of Congress), *Prairie Settlement: Nebraska Photographs and Family Letters, 1862–1912*, http://

memory.loc.gov/cgibin/query/h?ammem/psbib:@field%28docid+@lit %28p10002%29%29.

46. Sandoz, *Old Jules*, 116.

47. Sandoz, *Old Jules*, 183.

48. Checkoway, "Mail-order Brides,"332.

49. Checkoway, "Mail-order Brides," 332.

50. Riley, *Building and Breaking Families in the American West*, 14.

51. Sandoz, *Old Jules*, 3.

52. Sandoz, *Old Jules*, 98.

53. Sandoz, *Old Jules*, 101.

54. Sandoz, *Old Jules*, 102.

55. Sandoz, *Old Jules*, 166.

56. Sandoz, *Old Jules*, 207.

57. Sandoz, *Old Jules*, 167.

58. Sandoz, *Old Jules*, 114, 229.

59. Sandoz, *Slogum House*, 99.

60. Johannsen, "Meaning of Manifest Destiny," 13.

4. Typical pioneer sod home, Nebraska. Madrid Collection 200601400095.
Mari Sandoz High Plains Heritage Center.

The natural elements of rain, snow, hail, wind, and sun are petulant
and unpredictable actors in the drama for survival in the Sandhills.
In one of her earliest short stories, "The Vine," Mari Sandoz explores
the impact of extended drought on a couple who left the lush, green
lands of Indiana to homestead in the semiarid region of northwest
Nebraska. Telling the story of deprivation through the wife's perspective,
Sandoz delves into women's experiences in a more nuanced and mul-
tidimensional way than had other historians at that time. "The Vine" is
followed by Lisa Pollard's gendered analysis of Sandoz's story, proving
compelling insights and encouraging readers to consider drought, or
the withholding of a vital resource, as both reality and metaphor, and
its impact on shaping intimate relationships.

2

The Vine

MARI SANDOZ

The hill north of the little soddy rose tall and steep. Diagonal cow-paths, grassing over, marked it into a regular pattern from foot to sand-capped top. Soapweeds clustered about the highest dune, catching the first late winter sun. Perhaps the wind drove them over, like sheep, before the stinging sand, Baldwin had said. Meda couldn't see anything in that. She didn't see much in anything in Baldwin's world. She liked green things, like the glory vine.

Meda couldn't see the narrow valley, wrinkled plush of russet bunchgrass between the lower chophills with the wind ruffling the pile as it fitfully passed. She saw the greedy thirst of the long strip of gray that had been green corn in June. She didn't hear the coughing of the wind across the valley. She heard the crackle and snap of dry stems whipped by skeleton leaves.

Meda loved thick, green things like the glory vine that covered the window of the gray soddy and reached ambitiously toward the sod-covered eaves. The great heart-shaped leaves bobbed on their slender stems in the wind.

Tall and spare, she held her faded blue-checked apron back with one hand while she poured a dipper of water, brimming full, around the slender stalks, like tiny green pencils. The hungry sand soaked up the little pool, and as it vanished, Meda pushed dry sand over the wet spot from the edges with her broken shoe. She smoothed it over until it looked just as before—just as dry, just as yellow. Straightening up, she shaded her eyes and looked into the west, the northwest.

"There'll never be any rain," she told the vine. "I'll just have to water you." The thick leaves seemed to nod to her.

At the corners of the soddy, small holes, blowouts-to-be, spurted tiny volleys of sand as the wind playfully attacked the vine. Here and there a grain hit the window with a ping.

Standing in the whipping wind, Meda's body, in a long, faded, blue calico dress, looked hungry. Her hair, faded, straggled in the wind like raveled ends of old, weathered rope. Her hazel eyes looked hungry too, only too hungry to be fed. The smoldering yellow flame that lurked in their depths was hunger itself. Baldwin had told her to be careful of too much sunlight.

The glare outdoors blinded Meda as she stepped through the low doorway but she didn't need to see. She knew every detail of that crude room. She found the rocker near the window and swayed gently back and forth; her toes, bare and brown as saddle leather through the gaping holes in her shoes, dug little holes in the sand. The yellow flame died from her eyes, lost in the green shade of leaves that filtered the flecks of sunlight on the sand floor about her.

Meda looked about the room, its bareness old, old and yet strikingly new. Not even Baldwin could deny the smallness of the place, nor its shabbiness. An old grocery box covered with a frilled newspaper held the washbasin. The water pail stood beside the box on the sand. Newspaper frills, yellowed, lined the clock shelf, empty now. A flour-sack curtain, bleached on the grass to a blue-white, shut in the bed. A tablecloth of newer, creamier squares covered the two-legged table fastened to the wall. The kitchen corner was Baldwin's pride. It was a pick-up, one pick-up stove, pick-up pipe and pick-up frying pan. Only a few things, like the coffee pot and the saucepan, had been bought.

Two chairs, legs sunken into the sand, completed the furniture. "Not much to dust," Baldwin had said. What mattered dust, thought Meda, the yellow flaring up in her eyes. Even the walls would be dust if there were no roots to bind them into blocks. She sat still, her hands clenching and unclenching in her lap.

She compared it all to her Indiana home. She saw the cool porch, the shade trees. She wanted to see the rolling lawns of the chief citizen. She missed the small church bickerings and the news and gossip of the Ladies' Aid. Baldwin made light of the rivalry of neighbors over the parlor sets and crayon portraits. He despised the jealousies of the "folks back home." He even laughed at her charities "across the tracks," calling them inadequate, and he never could be dragged to a bazaar. Meda doted on these pastimes. She delighted in the slumming among what Baldwin termed "the unwashed." She felt she had lost her husband in this desert of soapweeds. He believed in the somnolent hills; he was a part of the simplicity, their strength. She thought resentfully of his frank enjoyment of their isolation.

Meda had felt nobly self-sacrificing when she came west with Baldwin. She had known they would soon go back home. But they hadn't, somehow, and now she hated it all. She hated the cold, she hated the heat. Blizzards, objects of wonder and delight to Baldwin, were days of disgust and loneliness to Meda. Not even the Indian summers nor the chinooks moved her. She cried for the cool green of the bluegrass meadows, never seeing the lovely, ever-changing browns and yellows of the hills.

A passionate fondness for green things grew on Meda. They made her think of Indiana. Crisp, green things, alien to the sun-yellowed hills. There had been a tall geranium that bore gorgeous red blossoms. A fall in the January mercury ended that. She had almost died; Baldwin had looked worried until spring brought the glory vine, with its deep red funnels against the slick, dark leaves. The red funnels died young; there was never any dew for them to catch, only heat, sun, and wind.

Meda had to admit she felt the hills, not like Baldwin, who felt a companionship in the purple hazes and the fiery evening sun. She feared the relentlessness of their long, lonesome days. But the nights were worse! Conversation was a skeleton of bones picked dry. She might look at the stars with Baldwin but they burned so far away. In the winter they were cold white lights mocking her from a blue steel sky. Meda hated them, as if they stood between her and the family circle where her brothers had always been frankly bored, but where her eyes hadn't burned, searing. . . .

Once, long ago, she had hated rain, too. It mussed the kitchen so, but now she would welcome it if any ever came. Then there was the cream and butter and fried chicken on Sundays or when the minister called. Meda remembered telling Baldwin that beans, always beans, palled so. He had replied, "They're a sure-fire crop."

Meda thought of dinner. She stepped out to squint at the sun. She saw windows of dancing heat waves over the dunes south of the soddy. A tiny, puffball cloud of dust trailed its thin tail down the narrow strip of corn along the north slope. The crop looked even grayer than before. Nearer and nearer came the cloud until a team and then a man could be seen, the nucleus of the cloud. Baldwin walked, carefully jerking the handles of the corn plow to left and right. Meda knew the leaves of the small plants would rattle against the rusty wheels.

Back in the room, Meda lit the fire. Cowchips from the old candy pail (another pick-up) and a handful of hay roared up the rusty pipe. The woman lifted a black kettle of beans from the oven. She poured a dipper of water over them. There would be soup again. Meda set the kettle on to boil. She never did like soup; she didn't like beans, either, but hunger would be appeased, even if it could demand only beans.

Baldwin could be heard outside. The snapping of the tugs in place across the horses' backs and the clatter of rings as the neckyoke dropped made Meda hurry. Baldwin came stooping through the doorway. His overalls were covered with dust. His blue eyes looked strangely light, like milky water, against his dirt-caked face. The long hair under his greasy Stetson was bleached to a taffy color with a frost of gray dust on it. Meda did not look up. She was busy poking chips into the cookstove. Her face was red with heat and her eyes reflected the leaping yellow flames as she broke the fuel into small pieces. There was a curl of distaste on her lip even though her hands were hidden with mammoth cotton gloves.

MARI SANDOZ

Baldwin poured out a scant cup of water. It rattled in the tin basin. He dipped his hands and rubbed his grimy face. Streaks of water ran down his neck in little rivulets. Pawing blindly along the wall, he grabbed the towel from its nail and rubbed it into his eyes. When he was through he ruefully surveyed the wreck. There wasn't a clean thread left. Meda, slipping off the gloves, saw the towel. She bit her lip, the yellow flames under her lashes danced. Baldwin held it out from him awkwardly.

"Never mind, Old Girl, I'll take them all to Twin Mills and wash them, next time I go."

Meda did not answer. She set the two bowls of soup upon the table and poured the coffee. Baldwin stood for a minute, looking at her, a little furrow between his brows. Then he set his large frame to the ridiculous table.

"Think that breeze will blow up something, Meda. I saw a swamp swallow skim the valley just before I came in." Baldwin salted his soup and broke little pieces of bread into the bowl.

Meda sat still, looking at the man "I don't believe it can rain. It never does here. It's the going without water that is more than I can bear."

Baldwin looked up surprised. "'Taint my fault it don't rain, or that the well went dry, is it? I'm no crazier than you about being just dampened 'stead of washed."

"It's not only the well." Meda's hands made a sweep of all the vast hills. "Three years of drouth, no corn, nothing but beans, beans. Is this what I left my home for? This—?"

She pushed her bowl back and, rising quickly, left the room. She stood outside, beside the window, her head touching the glory vine. The yellow flames in her eyes died sullenly down, like an ugly serpent before its charmer.

Baldwin ate steadily on. Meda heard the scraping of his spoon in the bottom of the dish and his cup being set down. After a few minutes she saw his pale blue eyes looking out between the leaves. They look clouded, hurt. Well, she had been hurt too; just wait until he got numb. The flames flickered and flared up as Baldwin appeared at the door.

"Meda, you've said all that before but what can I do? Rain may come any day and fill the water hole, yes, and water that damned vine of yours."

Baldwin strode to the window and jerked away a leaf.

"Drouth don't seem to hurt it much. Probably gets my drinking water."

"No, no, I only give it dishwater, only dishwater." Meda shrank against the rooty sod beside the window. Her eyes gleamed orange.

"So? Only dishwater? And how much is that? Remember, I'm not skinning my horses, hauling water over seven miles of sand for you to drown dishes in."

Baldwin's lips had gone white. Meda watched as he viciously turned the corner of the shack. The yellow flames leaped and danced in her eyes. She flew to the corner in time to see Baldwin lift the heavy lids by their crosspieces from one barrel, then the other. He peered into the last and his jaw dropped. He slammed the lid down with a curse.

"Not even a gallon left and they ought to be half full."

Meda took a step backwards, then another. Not only had she lost her husband but he had turned enemy. Baldwin lifted the spade from its hook among the tools along the sod wall. Without looking at Meda he passed her and sank the blade deep into the soil at the roots of the vine. Meda's eyes grew round yellow flames, cold, hard. Her hands dropped limp as Baldwin stooped to snatch up a handful of the turned-up soil. He squeezed it and let it fall, a firm oval ball with deep finger creases.

"Soaked!" He looked at Meda. "Soaked, and I skimp myself and my horses while you . . ." Anger snapped in his pale opal eyes. He made one vengeful thrust at the base of the vine with the spade. Straightening up, he looked slowly at Meda. She was watching him, her hands covered, shielded in her apron. Baldwin walked stiffly to hang the spade in its place. Meda did not move or speak. Baldwin stood before her, expecting something, but she was puzzled. What could he expect? She had seen him angry before but usually he did something foolish before it melted.

Meda stood still as Baldwin led the horses to the wagon. With a rattle of rings and snap of teeth on bit the hitching up went on. Meda caught Baldwin looking at her over Old Bluche's back as he untied the lines. Circling the team around the soddy, Baldwin was out of sight. Two heavy thumps and he appeared from the north side with the two water barrels, blackened from sun and rain, in the wagon. Rusty hoops held down the flapping canvas squares that kept the lids on.

Baldwin kept looking back, over his shoulder, as he started down the valley. Standing up, feet wide apart, he flipped the lines and the team stepped up. His shout, "Be back before dark," came clearly above the bump-bump of the empty barrels as the wheels hit the bunchgrass. The wagon rattled across the valley and began its upward climb through the sandy pass toward Twin Mills. Meda stood at the door, looking slowly all around the valley, her narrow horizon.

There was nothing to see. Heat waves danced over the rolling chophills every day. Tiny whirlwinds often chased each other across the narrow field. She didn't see the corn blades, rising and dipping, merrily whirling upward and dipping again. They finally settled slowly into the tawny grass and the fickle winds left them and hurried on to find other playmates.

Meda turned from the heat and glare. Her eyes, resting on the solid green thatch of the vine, became hazel again. She held one of the leaves, cool even in the withering sun, between her hot palms. The larger leaves drooped a little; the sun was too hot for them, thought Meda, as she pushed the lump of soil Baldwin had lifted back into the hole with her foot. Stepping on it easily, she tamped it back level with the earth.

The sun drove her indoors and she cleared away the dinner dishes. There was no water to wash them, so she stacked them in the empty black kettle and threw a dish towel over them to keep out the flies. She wondered vaguely if there would be a letter next freight day. She always wondered that, but no one ever wrote any more. Why should they? Mail once a month discouraged correspondence easily with a piqued family who didn't believe in Baldwin or in homesteading.

Then, too, there was seldom any respectable stationery, and so the months slipped by and it was now a year since she had written to anyone. There was nothing to say. The struggle to ignore the winter's blizzard or the summer's heat left her with no news. She moved her hands, one over the other, as she swayed in the rocker. The fire, yellow and fierce, burned her eyeballs. She thought it was the sun, too. The sand crunched softly under the rockers, falling from the wood back into the trenches in fine streams.

The sun did not fleck the ground now. Crystal clear blue sky showed between the transparent leaves, like green veined glass. Meda resented the blue. There was too much blue, too much sky. If the whole sky could be green—that green of the leaves, seen from the inside of the room. Then she wouldn't have to look at the blue spots that made her eyes burn. She could look at the green. Somehow now she *had* to look at the sky; even closing her eyes didn't help much. She could see the blue over the rolling dunes that turned to blue and purple in the distance, turning all to blue where they met the sky. She tried to imagine her home, the apple orchard down the slope from the house, but the blues and purples and golden tans of the hills crept between, especially the blues.

Meda opened her eyes. There it was, blue, blue. Why, there was more blue than there had been, more than there was green, and the green looked brown, even gray!

Stumbling through the door, she ran to the vine and touched one of the leaves. It was limp. Another crumbled in her hands, almost powdery. She opened her palms and watched the wind blow the bits from them until all of the leaf was gone. The yellow flames leaped and danced in her unblinking eyes.

She flew into the house and carried the water pail to the plant. Upsetting it at the roots, Meda waited. Time would not go. The water seemed to stand, a little pool of blue sky. She crushed another leaf.

The pool was still there, still blue. The leaves turned yellow, then gray. The pool was gone but the vine didn't grow fresh. The leaves began to rattle in the hot wind.

Meda stood very, very still. She wished the sky weren't so blue, it made her eyes burn. Suddenly she fell to her knees. She dug under the dry, crackling leaves, her hands clumsy with fear. She found it! The flame burned her; she buried her head in the leaves, the cut stalks in her palms. Her head dropped to her knees. The tendrils of the plant released the strings that held them and fell across her hair. Meda did not move.

A fan-shaped cloud hung in the northwest, gray and thin. It grew darker, slowly spreading its transparent fringe until the sun showed through, a white, round ball, without light. The cloud thickened, spread until the sun was gone. The rain began easily, a drop here and there. Then it stopped. The sand lay yellow with darker splotches, like freckles, but in a moment they were gone. Baldwin clucked up his team. They raised their heads and swung into a long stride that made the water barrels splash merrily. Baldwin looked at them and pulled the horses back to their slow walk. He sat sideways on the board used for a seat, turning his back to the rain that began again. Dusk stole down the gullies. The hills moved away in the darkness. The smell of wet horses came to his nostrils. He moved his foot and it struck a rusty syrup pail under the seat. He hoped Meda wouldn't mind too much when she saw what he had brought to replace the vine. He smiled into the darkness as he recalled how the greasy-looking woman at the cook house had gaped. Nesters weren't so popular at Twin Mills and here was one who wanted geranium slips! Well, he had them and a rooted wax plant "to boot."

Baldwin stripped the harness from the horses and turned them loose. He was soaked but he didn't mind. Water! and there might even be corn! He dug under the wagon seat for the syrup pail. As he lifted it he noticed that there was no light and there should have been a little, even through the vine and the rain. Perhaps Meda was asleep, he decided. Pail under arm, he went to the house. He felt for the knob, and didn't find anything, only a gap. Stepping nearer, he tried again. His hand struck the jamb. The door was open. He walked in and called softly, "Meda." No answer came and he called again, louder. His hands shook as he felt for a match. The first one sputtered, wet. The second match flared up and the darkness fell back. The wind whipped the flame and, shielding it with his cupped hand, he looked around the room. He took two steps to the bed and pulled back the white curtain. Both pillows sat up against the pine headboard, smooth and prim.

Baldwin lit the swinging bracket lamp and looked all about the room. The wick smoked; a black smudge grew up from one corner and spread over the globe to its fluted top. He stumbled over the pail of geranium slips in the doorway. He called "Meda" loudly, hands to his lips. There was a dim echo from the rain, nothing more.

Then he saw her crouched at the window. The vine had fallen all about her. The light came through the window clearly now, making little glittery streaks of the rain as it fell on the head of the woman.

He ran to her and lifted her in his arms, begging her to say what was the matter. She didn't answer, only whispered, always whispered. Baldwin set her into the rocker, trying to catch a word, but he couldn't. He pulled frantically at her knotted shoestring.

"Meda, are you sick? Meda, answer me."

She didn't notice him, but looked down at her hands full of the withered, soggy vine. Her lips moved and still Baldwin could not hear. He raised her face in his palm and his eyes went black with horror. In the lamplight her eyes roamed over his unknowingly, glowing like deep orange caves, alive with fierce, intense flames. She shrank down into the rocker like a frightened rabbit, clutching the vine to her breast.

"Who are you? You can't take my vine, my pretty green vine, you with the blue face."

Baldwin drew back, his hands clenched and white-knuckled. He tripped over the syrup pail with the rooted wax plant. It rolled away, spilling geranium slips over the sand.

3

The Gender of Drought in Mari Sandoz's "The Vine"

LISA POLLARD

Mari Sandoz's "The Vine" is the story of what happened when two settlers migrated onto the Great Plains from Indiana and established a sod home during a period of sustained drought, most likely in the late 1880s or early 1890s. The dry-ness on the plains is reflected in and amplified by the deepening drought of their relationship. Conversations between the two main characters, Meda and Baldwin, had become "a skeleton of bones picked dry."[1]

Meda planted a glory vine to remind her of her lush Indiana home. Baldwin sank a spade into the vine's roots and unearthed it when he noticed that Meda had been using hauled water instead of dish water to keep it alive. When Baldwin spoke, Meda's eyes flared "like an ugly serpent before its charmer."[2] Baldwin, as oblivious to Meda's flaming eyes as he was to her needs, left the soddy to haul more water from his not very handy source seven miles away.

5. Mary Sandoz and her children (*left to right*), Jules Jr., James, and Mari, 1900. Helen Winter Stauffer Collection 200300100032. Mari Sandoz High Plains Heritage Center.

When Baldwin returned with water and a geranium, he found a dark house and finally Meda in a corner wrapped in the limp glory vine. The few scholars who have written about the story have taken it literally and assumed that Meda was insane by the end, though it is unclear whether Meda was insane or had simply withdrawn herself from Baldwin's world and wrapped herself in the things that sustained her, rejecting Baldwin's vision of the West and all it entailed.[3] No scholar has questioned Baldwin's sanity. This essay argues that in "The Vine," Mari Sandoz, then Marie Macumber, engaged drought on the Great Plains as a deeply gendered event that shaped and redefined relationships in the family and between the Great Plains and the East. She also threw down the gauntlet for what was to follow in her later works, a complex western history, peopled by characters who subverted the stereotype and wrestled the communicative divide.

Mari Sandoz was ahead of her time when she engaged the relationship between gender and drought on the Great Plains. Walter Prescott Webb, writing in 1931, attributed women's insanity on the plains to the land. The Great Plains, he said, "mysterious, desolate, barren, and grief stricken—oppressed the women, drove them to the verge of insanity in many cases, as the writers of realistic fiction have recognized." Continuing, he argued that the Great Plains "repelled women" as much as they attracted men.[4] Webb then noted a vigorous body of literature filled with women's distrust and fear of the plains. The plains, he argued, "precluded the little luxuries that women love"—the wind, the sand, and the drought just overwhelmed them with a sense of desolation, futility, and insecurity.[5] Women, he claimed, because of their scarcity, were "very dear and were much sought after, prized and protected by every man."[6] Mari Sandoz, on the other hand, understood scarcity in the social construction of the heterosexual nuclear family and understood the most intimate manifestations of drought, hunger, and longing frequently belonged to the family on the Great Plains. She understood that drought reshaped gender and family dynamics. Drought in its physical sense refers to a long period of dryness, but drought in its metaphorical sense—a long period of the absence of something much desired—is clear throughout the story. Sandoz also knew the full range of women's responses to life on the Great Plains, much as she studied and acknowledged a range of constructions of masculinity.

Mari Sandoz had experienced the impact of a period of prolonged drought in relationships in her life. Historian John R. Wunder noted Mari struggled throughout her early years for access to an education. She was blinded in one eye and almost died catching cattle for her family in a blizzard on the Great Plains. She acquired her teaching certificate and hence a step along the road to independence without her father's knowledge. She came to the university despite his violent opposition. Indeed, her father, Jules Ami Sandoz, considered writers to be the maggots of the world. Mari's mother, like Mari, endured physical abuse from her father, and she worked tirelessly while Jules pursued his visions for the plains and later Canada or Mexico.[7] When Mari's mother refused to sell their Nebraska property and move to Canada during what Jules Sandoz Jr. described as one of Jules Sandoz's "damn the government spells," he strangled her. Jules Sandoz Jr. wrote: "One day I heard a ruckus in the house and ran down from the barn to look. Papa had Mama by the throat up against the wall, choking her. She was blue in the face and shaking, limp like a rag doll. I screamed as loud as I could that he was killing my Mama, and it got his attention. I thought he was going to come after me next, but he let go, and she crumpled to the floor in a heap."[8] Meda's eyes in "The Vine" shoot flames at Baldwin; but in *Old Jules*, Mary's eyes reflect "all the resentment of years' accumulation murking her eyes to a stony gray," causing others to think that "somebody ought to talk to Jules" as "one woman in the insane asylum was enough."[9]

Over the years, Mari encountered many women who went insane on the Great Plains during periods of drought and could have served as models for Meda, but it was rarely the land alone that precipitated that change. Throughout the sustained drought on the Great Plains in the late 1880s and early 1890s, settlers embraced mysticism and powder to bring rain. In her essay "Nebraska Rain Making and Rain Lore," Louise Pound described popular nineteenth-century rainmaking theories.[10] James P. Espy, meteorologist to the War Department, thought large prairie fires could bring rain.[11] Edward Powers proposed a concussion theory. Panhandle settlers formed a "Rain God Association" to procure funds for gunpowder to blast the clouds, their thinking followed along the lines of blowing the rain out of the sky if it wouldn't come down of its own accord.[12] Rainmakers and revivals were common. In *Old Jules*, Mrs. Schmidt, who had eight children and a husband, sang all the way home from one such revival and wound up in the insane asylum at Norfolk the next week.[13] Elise, Cousin Pete's wife, also in *Old Jules*, went to Norfolk after her husband kicked her until she almost bled to death. Dick Weyant commented: "That family shore is tough on womenfolks."[14] Old Jules, with his mouth stuffed full of Mary Sandoz's sausage and bread offered: "Seems to me that all the women are a little crazy."[15]

Henriette Sandoz, Jules Sandoz's second wife, might also have been a possible model for Meda. Henriette went insane, but not before divorcing Jules after the Niobrara cattle feuds. Jules brought Henriette onto the Great Plains from Boston where she taught French and manners in a private home. His sister Elvina introduced the two through letters. In 1887 Henriette came west to Rushville. She spent her first night on the Great Plains with Jules in a leaky shack, which he borrowed as a step up from his dugout. The shack was full of mud, traps, and guns, and he'd forgotten to buy kerosene, so they ate crackers and cheese by the light of the cook stove. Morning found Henriette sitting on the bed with an umbrella over her head; the minute Jules left the shack, Henriette tore Elvina's letter of introduction up and threw it in the fire. Henriette was determined to make the best of it, so she laid her own claim and built a house that was fit to live in. Jules moved right in, until the

38   LISA POLLARD

end of the Niobrara feud when Henriette threw all his guns and traps in the road and went to Rushville to divorce him.

Six years of Jules's fighting with the cattle barons and the property insecurity from extended court battles apparently drove Henriette over the edge. After the divorce, she wound up at the asylum at Norfolk, returned, encountered the community and then purportedly went insane again. The symptoms of her insanity—hair flying wild, running at hecklers with a raised knife, and living in a cave—make it clear she had lost her grasp on reality. Men, such as Baldwin and later Old Jules, frequently engaged in risky enterprises that brought trouble to themselves and their households without being deemed insane. Mari's own marriage to Wray Macumber, whom she divorced in 1919 for extreme cruelty, could also have served as a model for "The Vine." Jules Sandoz Jr., describing a trip that Jules Sandoz took with the Macumber family to Lincoln in 1917, wrote, "Papa said Wray swore at my sister at every gate because she didn't seem to be opening and shutting them as fast as he liked. But most men swore at their wives, so that was not considered unusual."[16]

When "The Vine" was published, it ended an earlier period of drought in Mari Sandoz's writing career. Dorothy Ann Switzer, a University of Nebraska classmate who later wrote about Mari, remembered Mari telling her, "I'm just as much of an oddity as ever, but now I'm the oddity who has a story published."[17] Mari, according to Switzer, "received considerable recognition from faculty members and fellow students" after the story was published.[18] Mari had found a community of people in Lincoln who supported and furthered her writing work. When "The Vine" was first published in February of 1927, it became the first article in the first issue of the *Prairie Schooner*.[19] Helen Stauffer noted that before the *Schooner* published it, "The Vine" had been rejected by many eastern magazines. One editor told Mari he'd seen a surprising number of stories about women who went insane on the plains that year.[20] This editor might not have had an eye for satire. After "The Vine" was published, it immediately received national recognition. Edward J. O'Brien gave it a three-star rating on his Roll of Honor, the Best Short Stories of 1927, although the story was not published in the resulting O'Brien volume of twenty short stories, including lesser writers like Ernest Hemingway and Sherwood Anderson.[21] The success of her *Prairie Schooner* publication gave Mari confidence to move ahead. Mari was now a published author.[22]

Mari Sandoz wrote about "The Vine" differently at different points in her life. The year after "The Vine" was published, Mari described it as "the acutely painful story, represented by The Vine which pleased Mr. E. O'Brian sufficiently to bring my name on his Roll of Honor, if that means anything."[23] That was before the publication of *Old Jules*. In 1943 Emily Schossberger at the University of Nebraska Press wrote to Mari to request permission to republish "The Vine" in a *Prairie Schooner* retrospective anthology. Mari responded: "About The Vine—I've never liked the story as anything but satire and since I'm the only person who recognizes its satirical intention, I dislike having it published. However, since it was the first story in the first issue of the Schooner and so has some pertinency to the anthology, I don't object if you decide on that."[24]

As an "acutely painful story," or satire, or an "acutely painful" satire, the symbolism of "The Vine" is complex. The glory vine, like the red geraniums that came before, mattered differently to the main characters of the story, Meda and Baldwin, and they weren't able to communicate across those differences. Drought clarified the great divide. Mari Sandoz contrasted Meda and Baldwin's former home in Indiana with the Great Plains during a period of drought. Baldwin found opportunity and hope in the West; Meda saw nothing but deprivation and isolation. Meda kept the past alive and her sense of well-being by growing green things; her most recent green acquisition, the glory vine, sustained Meda's life on the Great Plains from day to day. It was a thin thread. The vine reminded her of all the things she left behind: Indiana, her family's home, the "cool porch," the shade trees, the bluegrass meadows, the rolling lawns, her church. The vine connected Meda to the past, a past that mattered to her. It connected her to her work through the Ladies' Aid Society with the people who Baldwin termed "the unwashed" of the world. It encompassed the companionship of friends and brothers. The vine connected Meda to a world in Indiana where food scarcity hadn't been a daily issue, where there was cream, butter, and fried chicken to be had, rather than Baldwin's "sure-fire crop" of daily beans.

Baldwin, on the other hand, had little use for the vine or the memories it connected Meda to. He "despised the jealousies of the 'folks back home.'" He "laughed at their charities across the tracks, calling them inadequate. Bazaars bored him."[25] He relished life on the Great Plains; it enhanced his sense of masculinity and independence. Baldwin, we were told, felt a companionship to the fiery sun and purple hazes. He, unlike Meda, experienced mobility in "The Vine," leaving the soddy daily to work in the field, haul water, or take their clothes to Twin Mills for washing. Meda's day-to-day life on the plains was confined to the sod house. Back East, she had both mobility and family. In the soddy on the plains, she talked to the vine for most of the day. When Baldwin sinks a spade into the glory vine's roots, it's the final straw; he literally spaded both the past and the present that sustained Meda.

The vine may have been Mari's satirical twist on the vine in John 15:5–8: "I am the vine; you are the branches. If you remain in me and I in you, you will bear much fruit; apart from me you can do nothing. If you do not remain in me, you are like a branch that is thrown away and withers; such branches are picked up, thrown into the fire and burned. If you remain in me and my words remain in you, ask whatever you wish, and it will be done for you. This is to my Father's glory, that you bear much fruit, showing yourselves to be my disciples." As an allegory for the relationship between the East and the West, the state of the vine demonstrated national dysfunction and the need for change, much like the many-headed hydra cartoons of the Populist movement depicting the Beast in the East.[26] The hydra of "The Vine" had a cow-chip head, a laundry head, and a dinner-of-beans head.

Baldwin's character was an early preview of the studies of gender and masculinity that would follow in stories from *Old Jules*. Between 1926 and 1927, about the same time as "The Vine," was published, Mari engaged in fieldwork in Lincoln, Nebraska, for an article entitled "The Stranger at the Curb," which she completed in late 1930 or early 1931.[27] Published posthumously in 1988 in the *Mid-American Review of Sociology*, "The Stranger at the Curb" is based on interviews with 385 men who wanted to pick Mari up on the streets of downtown Lincoln and near the state capitol building over the course of four years. When they'd stop, she'd pick up her notebook and interview them, keeping detailed notes in a tiny blue notebook that she purchased for just that purpose. The resulting article is a detailed and humorous study of the curb pickup habits of men. Curbers from every state in the union and three Canadian provinces are represented in her study. There was no drought of curbers. But Mari's early study of curbers, as did "The Vine," demonstrated her interest in gender as it developed relationally in the context of interactions between men and women.

Baldwin was as finely drawn as Mari's curbers, though not as fully developed as Old Jules. Mari Sandoz's portraits of men were always complex. Baldwin's redeeming feature is his love of the Great Plains. Baldwin's name comes from the Old High German word for "bold one." Baldwins were to be found among the crusaders and the first settlers in the English colonies. And our Baldwin lived up to his name, as sinking a spade in the roots of Meda's vine and unearthing it was indeed a bold and risky action that didn't work out so well for Baldwin the Bold—and oblivious. The phallic overtones are not to be missed, but it's a classic case of a misplaced signifier. Baldwin took great pride in the kitchen corner, which he'd put together from "pick-ups" for Meda to use daily; it consisted of a pick-up stove, pick-up pipe, and pick-up frying pan left by other settlers to the plains along their way West. "Not much to dust," said Baldwin when Meda confronted him about the starkness of their soddy.[28] Indeed, there was not too much to dust because everything was dust. Meda especially appreciated the Great Plains climate; she hated the cold, but blizzards were "objects of wonder for Baldwin."[29] Picked-up cow chips were Meda's primary source of fuel for the soddy; they made her lips curl. Baldwin lacked empathy for everything Meda experienced. When she told him, "It's the going without water that's more than I can bear," Baldwin said, "Taint my fault that it don't rain, or that the well went dry, is it? I'm no crazier than you about being just dampened instead of washed."[30]

Meda's name could have had multiple sources. The German name Meda means prophetess.[31] As a prophetess of things to come in relationships on the Great Plains, Meda's vision does not bode well for the connection between Meda and Baldwin or the connection between East and West. Mari could also have been drawing on classical tradition for the name Meda. In her "Letter for a Seventh Birthday," written for Clara Mae Curtis's birthday, Mari said that when she was just seven and all her work for the day was done and she had watched her brothers well to avoid beatings from Old Jules, she'd pull down his *History of the World* and read and look at the pictures. She knew all of the titles by heart and was especially skeptical of men like Caesar and Napoleon who "tried to grab the whole world."[32] Mari took courses in the classics at the University of Nebraska–Lincoln with Professor John Rice and, according to her biographer, especially delighted in the Greek tragedies.[33]

Hence, Meda might have been an abbreviation for Medea. Meda could also have been an abbreviation for Andromeda, daughter of the king and queen of Ethiopia who, according to the Greek mythmakers, was chained to a cliff and set to be sacrificed by her father to appease the sea god Poseidon. A last-minute rescue from Perseus thwarted Poseidon, and Andromeda was rewarded with the

MARRIAGE her father promised to Perseus. Andromeda became a star for keeping her promise; but marriage was no rescue in Mari Sandoz's "The Vine."[34]

Meda is also associated with snakes in "The Vine." Her eyes, we are told, flared at Baldwin "like an ugly serpent before its charmer." So perhaps Meda channeled Medusa, the Greek Gorgon whose hair spouts snakes. Gorgons, like Medusa, protected the ancient rituals and knowledge of Greek tradition, much as Meda protected her vision of the past. Mari Sandoz invoked the power of the snake throughout her early novels and short stories as a symbol for the writer, an individual who has the snake's knowledge and can end drought by placing the present and past in proper perspective, much as Mari Sandoz placed her life history and the history of the American West in proper perspective.

In Mari Sandoz's first novel after "The Vine," and predating *Old Jules*—*The Ungirt Runner*, later retitled *Murky River*—the main character, Endor, is terrified of snakes because they reminded her of a childhood locked in a cellar for punishment, much as Mari was locked in a cellar by Jules when she wrote her first short story for the *Omaha Daily News*.[35] However, by the publication of *Old Jules*, Mari had associated herself with a snake, as had her Grossmutter who, in *Old Jules*, found Mari sleeping with a sleeping snake in her lap. This event horrified Grossmutter who viewed it as an omen: "No good could come of this!"[36] "There was a warning for women in Genesis against snakes! This traffic was a mark of the devil's."[37] Snake, in the Judeo-Christian tradition, brings forbidden knowledge to women, ending intellectual drought. Snakes in the Hebrew tradition are associated with the power of divination, fertility, and fortune-telling. Moses's staff turns into a snake. Jules, who listened, thought there was "more sense to the Greek notion that snakes bring wisdom and healing."[38] When she was eleven, Mari and her brothers found another snake, and Mari was fascinated. Grossmutter said, "Ugly thing, you, stepping on the tail, still alive and then laughing. Are you bewitched?"[39]

Snakes are associated with knowledge in *Old Jules*; when Mary first learned about Henriette, Jules's second wife, the blanket she was folding "uncoiled like a thick snake."[40]

Meda's large cotton cow-chip gloves connected her to the much later Kinkaiders who Mari Sandoz described as in *Old Jules*:

> With no tree closer than the Niobrara River or the brush of the Snake, little money, and wretched roads over twenty miles of sun-drenched or snow-glazed hills to the nearest railroad, wood and coal were out of the question. Cow chips were the solution. Most of the settlers had lost all the qualms that curse the fastidiousness long before they reached the hills. Bare handed they took up the battle, braving rattlesnakes, which upon acquaintance failed to live up to their reputation for aggressiveness. City women encased their still white hands in huge gloves and, with repugnance no extremity could erase, endured the first few weeks somehow.[41]

Kinkaiders, however, frequently set up on the Great Plains alone. When they did, Old Jules, then in his fourth marriage to Mary, Mari's mother, preached the gospel of marital bliss as an engine of settlement on the Great Plains.[42] Sometimes women Kinkaiders set up housekeeping with other women, such as the retired high school instructor and music teacher from Boston, who were "a little afraid of their neighbors and of the rough-appearing men in boots and high hats who loped past or stopped for a drink at their wells."[43]

Returning to Walter Prescott Webb's thesis about women who went insane on the Great Plains, certainly they are to be found in Mari Sandoz's work. But the two Kinkaiders from Boston weren't on his radar, nor were the many other western women Mari Sandoz wrote about, like her mother, Mary. Mari Sandoz gave us a much more complicated picture of a gendered West, during periods of drought and beyond. It's a vision of the Great Plains where drought shaped and changed households as well as political dynamics and where dysfunction in the family shaped the region's development.

The highly drawn characters of "The Vine," Meda and Baldwin, would have resonated with Mari Sandoz's audience on both a satirical and acutely painful level. Sandoz hammered home what the United Nations continues to express in 2013: drought affects women's lives differently than men's, depending on their relationship to household production. When women are the water carriers, they walk further to carry water. When they are responsible for washing clothes, drought makes it harder to keep their families clean and hence forestall disease. Food and fuel scarcity impact women differently than men. But Sandoz also knew and portrayed the incredible strength and resilience of women and men on the plains, which is why "The Vine" functions equally well as satire for an East looking West.

NOTES

Mari Sandoz, "The Vine," in *Hostiles and Friendlies: Selected Short Writings of Mari Sandoz* (Lincoln: University of Nebraska Press, 1992), 117–25; first publication of the story under the pseudonym Marie Macumber, "The Vine," in *Prairie Schooner* 1, no.1 (January 1927): 7–16.

1. Sandoz, "The Vine," 119.
2. Sandoz, "The Vine," 119.
3. Johnson, "The Prairie Schooner: Ten Years," 71–82; Stauffer, *Mari Sandoz*, Western Writers Series, no. 63, 10.
4. Webb, *Great Plains*, 505.
5. Webb, *Great Plains*, 248.
6. Pifer and Sandoz Jr., *Son of Old Jules*, 82.
7. Throughout Sandoz's novel *Old Jules*, her father contemplated a Canadian settlement. Early in the novel he asked himself: "Had he chosen to come to America, America, the land of the free, to find that corruption followed upon the heels of settlers as wolves once trailed the buffalo herds. Must he keep moving always ahead, always alone? He would pack up for the wilds of Canada" (76). Later, convinced "the country was going to the dogs," Old Jules still hoped to build his planned community in Canada

or Mexico (278). Jules's moves counted on women and children's work, and he again considered starting a settlement in British Columbia, "where there would be good food, good wine, good talk, with strong women and sturdy children for the fork and the hoe" (345).

8. Pifer and Sandoz Jr., *Son of Old Jules*, 82.
9. Sandoz, *Old Jules*, 229.
10. Pound, "Nebraska Rain Lore and Rain Making."
11. Pound, "Nebraska Rain Lore and Rain Making,"131.
12. Pound, "Nebraska Rain Lore and Rain Making,"135.
13. Sandoz, *Old Jules*, 150.
14. Sandoz, *Old Jules*, 380.
15. Sandoz, *Old Jules*, 380.
16. Pifer and Sandoz Jr., *Son of Old Jules*, 105.
17. Switzer, "Mari Sandoz's Lincoln Years," 111.
18. Switzer, "Mari Sandoz's Lincoln Years," 111.
19. Stauffer, *Mari Sandoz, Story Catcher of the Plains*, 65.
20. Stauffer, *Mari Sandoz, Story Catcher of the Plains*, 65.
21. Stauffer, *Mari Sandoz, Story Catcher of the Plains*, 65.
22. Stauffer, *Mari Sandoz, Story Catcher of the Plains*, 65; Switzer, "Mari Sandoz's Lincoln Years," 107–15.
23. Stauffer, *Mari Sandoz, Story Catcher of the Plains*, 2.
24. Stauffer, *Mari Sandoz, Story Catcher of the Plains*, 194.
25. Sandoz, "The Vine," in *Hostiles and Friendlies*, 119.
26. Alabama Department of Archives and History Digital Collections, "Well, Brother, will you let the beast have your vote, too?," http://digital.archives.alabama.gov/cdm/ref/collection/photo/id/5285.
27. Sandoz, "Stranger at the Curb," 31–42.
28. Sandoz, "The Vine," 118.
29. Sandoz, "The Vine," 119.
30. Sandoz, "The Vine," 121.
31. Author's conversation with Christina Brantner, professor of German at the University of Nebraska–Lincoln, 2013.
32. Sandoz, "Letter for a Seventh Birthday," 287.
33. Stauffer, "Mari Sandoz and the University of Nebraska," 253.
34. Wikipedia, "Andromeda (mythology)," accessed June 2013, http://en.wikipedia.org/wiki/Andromeda_%28mythology%29.

35. Stauffer, *Mari Sandoz, Story Catcher of the Plains*, 67.
36. Sandoz, *Old Jules*, 216–17.
37. Sandoz, *Old Jules*, 216–17.
38. Sandoz, *Old Jules*, 217.
39. Sandoz, *Old Jules*, 250.
40. Sandoz, *Old Jules*, 189.
41. Sandoz, *Old Jules*, 359.
42. Sandoz, *Old Jules*, 359.
43. Sandoz, *Old Jules*, 359.

LISA POLLARD

6. Sandoz Farmstead, the Niobrara River Place, near Hay Springs, Nebraska. Birthplace of Mari Sandoz. Helen Winter Stauffer Collection 201001100085–2. Mari Sandoz High Plains Heritage Center.

Slogum House shocked readers with its portrayal of family values gone terribly wrong. Sandoz turns the familiar roles of women as self-sacrificing agents of morality upside down with her construction of the protagonist, Gulla Slogum. Reared in poverty, ignorance, and violence, Gulla mercilessly abuses her family and the law as she schemes to acquire middle-class status and respectability. Glenda Riley's essay follows and explores why Sandoz's innovative use of gender inversion proved so disturbing, considering as well the literary device as a critique of middle-class hypocrisy, and the destructive drive for power hidden behind the thin veneer of gentility.

4

Excerpt from *Slogum House*

MARI SANDOZ

The first rays of the morning sun shot, yellow and burning, over the crest of the hogback that stood dark against the sky. Although it was still May, the early heat of a dry summer scattered the line of little clouds riding low in the west, leaving the horizon wide and bare over the hard-land table of the upper Niobrara. In the rutted trails dust began to curl and run like twists of smoke from dying campfires. And on the ridge the sparse sand grass rattled a little along the path worn deep and loose by the habit of one man's feet.

Every day at this time Ruedy Slogum plodded up the steep, sandy slope and stood against the bright morning to look back upon Slogum House on the plain below. Then he went on, down the far side, his pace quickening. Sometimes he even ran a little, for the hillside was steep and pulled him foolishly.

Behind him Slogum House and its windmill, its sheds and pole corrals, huddled on the prairie like a gray wart in the pit of a worn and callused palm, drawing all the rutted trails of Oxbow Flat toward it. The house, a two-story block topped by a crow's nest not much larger than a smokehouse, was a patchwork of used lumber put together as it came, with no paint to hide its bastard origins. On the west end of the second story bare studding waited for the siding, and under a tarp in the straw cowshed, where no stranger was ever to go, lay a pile of new lumber, nailholed, but without the black streaks of rain on iron; midnight lumber, a Slogum purchase, as it was called—but guardedly, behind the palm. And in the deep canyon below the house lay four walls and a shingled roof of what had been the church of Pastor Zug on Cedar Flats yesterday evening.

Before the sun broke the far plain into a shimmer of heat dance, Libby, the eldest daughter of the Slogums, climbed to the crest of the hogback, her black cat running like a dog before her. Tall in her blowing skirts of yellow gingham, the girl looked down upon the empty trails of the plain spread before her. With her long hand to the brim of her sailor she searched the horizon, from the dark trees topping Cedar Canyon in the southwest, on past the deep, invisible oxbow of the Niobrara River to Sundance Table beyond, and to the feather of train smoke that smudged the sky over Dumur, twenty-five miles to the northeast.

Today she turned back to the line of blue-black trees that marked the bluffs of Cedar Creek. With her free hand on the signal cloth in her pocket, she watched the trail that crept out of the hazy southwest from the settlement of Pastor Zug, dipped into the Cedar Creek Canyon and up on this side, around Spring Slough and the west end of the hogback into sight of Slogum House.

But there was nothing of life on the shimmering horizon, nothing at all except the distant homestead buildings squatting like weary animals on the far sides of mirage lakes on the hot plain, and several rectangles that were the young groves of timber claims. Occasionally a dry-land whirlwind moved in a pillar of dust across a ploughed strip and then was lost on the nigger-wool sod, close-rooted enough to hold the soil in the longest drouth.

Once Libby turned from the settled tableland before her to the southeast, where a blurring sea of yellow-green sandhills hid growing ranches about the headwaters of Willow and Cedar creeks. But she looked nearer, down the slope of the hogback into the deep, timbered canyon of Spring Branch, its walls matted with wild roses in bloom, to where her father, Ruedy Slogum, worked in his gardens, his flowers and his fish ponds. She did it by a turn of her head over her shoulder, and swiftly, so swiftly that no watcher from Slogum House might see.

At last she pulled down the green veil of her hat, spread her skirt in a fan about her on the sandy ridge, and settled herself to watching the southwest, the signal cloth ready in her pocket. And away from her, no nearer than some curious wild animal might, sat her black tom, the tip of his tail nervous.

From the doorway of her room at Slogum House, Regula Slogum—Gulla, as she was called—watched her daughter on the hogback, the mother's little eyes half buried in the flesh of her broad face, but ready to catch the first movement of the black cloth signal. And in the meantime she rocked her body, so like a keg in its dressing sacque over a drawstring petticoat, or tipped herself forward to find her lean mouth in a small hand glass while she plucked at the dark fringe of hair on her upper lip.

And every fifteen minutes or so the woman laid down the tweezers and plodded heavily upstairs to look out between the bare studding of the west side over Oxbow Flat to see that its trails were really empty. Satisfied, she went back, her felt soles soft as the padded feet of a heavy animal on the rag runner of her room, back to her watching and the tweezers and the glass.

While Gulla and her daughter were on the lookout, the two elder Slogum sons, Hab and Cash, sprawled on their bed upstairs, their cartridge belts heavy about their clothed bodies, their boots handy, sleeping away the day in compensation for the labors of the night. Down the hall, beyond the freighters' bunk room, lay the two extra girls imported from Deadwood to free the Slogum daughters of the unimportant ranch hands that would be thick on the trails until the snow came and the roads were blocked for winter. The girls slept heavily, for the night had been a busy one with them, too. And in the third-story crow's nest the yellow, dusty shaft of sunlight from a peephole moved down the opposite wall in a bright golden dot. Unnoticed, it touched the stubble-whiskered man hunched forward upon a box—another Slogum hide-out, as the settlers called them, suspecting more than they knew. Slowly the spot of light crept down the holster hanging from the man's hip and away across the bare floor and the white chamber pot covered with a stained magazine.

But no prying bar of sun could disturb the cool first-floor room of Annette and Cellie, the twin daughters of Slogum House. In the green-blinded duskiness, the twenty-year-olds, supposed to be asleep, whispered the foolish words of their lovers between them and laughed softly as they lay with squares of flannel dipped in sweet milk upon their faces, for at Slogum House, as elsewhere, beauty is a precious thing.

A long time Libby Slogum examined the horizon through the green of her chiffon veil that lent a springlike freshness to the dry, hard-land table of the upper Niobrara country, almost as though there had been snow that winter of ninety-four and five, or rain in April. There was no movement on the far plain, and on Oxbow nothing but the slow roll of a tumbleweed, freed in a shift of wind from the line fence and zigzagging over the Flat like a wandering sheep. At Slogum House the windmill turned with a faint plump-plump, spouting hesitating water into the stilted supply tank, also a Slogum purchase. The mill had belonged to a homesteader with ranching ambitions in a hay flat down east a ways, until he shot himself in the back. There was a lot of talk about it out at the breaking and around the hog pens of the newer settlers. How could a man shoot himself so, and without powder burns?

But it had happened before, often, in the range country. The Bar UY outfit got their meadow back and let the improvements stand for the use of their hay crews. Long before haying time the place was cleaned of everything but the cylinder hole. The windmill got damaged some in the long snaking with a log chain over the hills to Slogum House and took a lot of greasing, but with the supply tank from Brule painted over, and piping gathered up here and there, Gulla had running water pretty cheap.

When Libby was certain that no ridge or gully hid what she was sent to discover, she took her tight little ball of knitting from her pocket and began another round of fern-leaf insertion for the ruffle of Annette's Fourth of July petticoat. The slim steel needles in her fingers were so swift that the sun scarcely caught a glint from the metal as she worked. And every few minutes the finger guiding the delicate thread stopped erect as the girl looked away into the southwest.

The nooning sun that drove the shadows of the soapweeds into the protection of their sharp spears burned down on the girl's head. But she preferred the heat to the shade of Cellie's plaid silk parasol, a present from old eagle-beak Judge Puddley. Gulla had wanted Libby to take it. A little hot sun on the back might not hurt anybody, but it helped turn the skin of a lady to cowhide, she scolded. The girl gave her mother no reply, only a slow look from her narrow green eyes, and so the woman let her go. Like a white pig in a hog wallow, not get-up enough to climb out. Like all the Slogums.

By the time the faint tones of Gulla's dinner bell came up the ridge, several horsebackers and creeping teams had moved along the slow, dusty trails to the Slogum yard. Usually the men stopped, perhaps to feed and water and eat, and then pushed on. When the last horse was gone from the hitching rack, the silent little Babbie, Gulla's new kitchen help from the home for wayward girls, climbed up the hogback, the sun bright on the syrup bucket she carried. Putting the lunch down beside Libby, she went to sit alone among the dark clumps of soapweeds straggling up the ridge, even farther away than the black cat.

While Libby ate she watched the girl between the slitted lids of Slogum House. Babbie sat motionless, dead, her tear-faded blue eyes on the sand before her, not seeing the panting lizard in the shade of a soapweed or the lone grouse flying over the hogback to her nest in the bunch grass of the hills. The shirring of wings and the soft cackling were a friendly noise in the stillness.

Once the girl rubbed her water-roughened hands over each other, probably thinking of the baby she had to give away. Then she was still again, not even noticing the cat ignore a bit of beef thrown to him. At last Libby rolled her fringed napkin into its ring and mousey little Babbie carried the syrup pail back again, down the steep slope.

When she was gone, Libby got up to stretch her legs, stalking the crest of the hogback tall and straight against the whitish sky of midday, where the mother could see her from Slogum House, and Ruedy, the father, too. He was probably hoeing in his garden or resting under the slim young cottonwoods in Spring Branch Canyon and eating his dinner from another syrup pail, his pet antelope in the shade beside him. And on the windy hogback that stood between the range country and the settlers of the hard-land region, between the man and the woman of Slogum House, this daughter walked free and aloof, her black tom leaping along beside her, always too far and too wild for touching.

When the sun's rays lost their worst sting, Cellie, the plumper of the twins, came out into the wind of the Slogum yard in her flying red dress to hang out a row of starched, gleaming white underthings: foamy petticoats, ruffly corset covers, and, demurely away from the road but perfectly visible, the embroidery-and-lace-trimmed split drawers. Usually at this time of day the twins took their horses out, alone or with some of their admirers, toward the timbered Niobrara, always riding astride, the one public lapse from her notion of what ladies might do that the mother permitted the twins. Sidesaddles were so dangerous on these wild Western horses, she sometimes said as she saw them go, the well-fed young colts crowhopping a little, fine necks bowed, bits foaming. Actually it was because the twins were more conspicuous astride, showing off their white shirtwaists and their smooth-fitting divided Skirts. Even settlers between their plough handles turned to look after them.

But to-day the twins must remain at Slogum House, for there might be trouble, trouble involving men, and therefore the line of snowy wash and the girls who wore these things should be useful.

All day Libby had watched the southwest, but because the trails from the settlement of Pastor Zug were bare as a sheep range the girl gradually let her eyes wander with any movement on Oxbow Flat below her, if nothing more than the slow bounce of a jackrabbit. Once, when she followed the gliding shadow of an eagle hanging against the light sky, she noticed a freight outfit coming fast around the northeast end of the hogback, along the Willow Creek road. Probably Old Moll's white mules, the finest hauling outfit in the country, with either Moll or her hired man on the bedroll roped to the running gears. Two of the mules Moll raised herself and had to care for at the livery barns, since the time one of them kicked the hat off a man who tried to help her hitch up.

Libby watched the light outfit come, stirring up a trail of dust that moved in a low wall across the Flat. If it was the woman herself she would head directly for the Niobrara and camp out, always with a little extra grub in the box for, perhaps, the Masterson children, who might come to look shyly from the bushes as she laid out her lunch. Or perhaps for some horsebacker, traveling far and light.

Libby ate with the woman once, when she had been plumming, several years before. "Aw, hell, just forget you're a Slogum," Moll told her when she hung back. "You can't let it stand between you and everybody all your life. Eat."

So she ate, spearing bacon from the frying pan with an old iron fork and envying the lean, pepper-gray woman in her denim skirt and high, laced boots. She even envied her the last name, made up from her brand for the filing papers to her homestead—Barheart. Old Moll was very open about it, saying she had kicked her past in the pants and come West, like most of the other settlers, only they wouldn't own up like she did.

So while the smooth, cream-white mules rolled their corncobs around on the grass that day, Libby Slogum ate bacon and buns and drank coffee with lots of sugar in it from a tin cup beside Old Moll. And around them the vagrant October wind swirled drying leaves into little piles, and the old cottonwood above them dropped fresh, golden-yellow ones, bitter-fragrant, into their laps.

It was Old Moll to-day, all right. The four mules swinging along abreast were headed toward the Niobrara ford, along the old trail across Oxbow that Gulla had closed with a four-wire fence and hung with torn underwear at the rain-gutted old ruts. No one else, not even the sheriff, would dare take down a Slogum fence.

The sudden boom of a shotgun brought Libby guiltily to her feet, her ball of thread rolling away into the sand. But everything was quiet enough down at Slogum House. Evidently it was only Ruedy shooting a hawk or maybe a rattlesnake in the sunny rocks above his gardens. The southwest was still empty, with no black knot of men following the trail over which the walls and the roof of a church came the night before.

By the time Libby was settled with her knitting again a piece of the western horizon line thickened, separated from the sky, and spread until it was a gray-brown blanket creeping toward the river—more Wyoming stock, burnt out by the settler-cattleman wars and the drouth, coming into the hills. Gulla wouldn't like it, Libby knew. But she'd give them pasture in Spring Slough for the night, charge them well for it, and plan for the day when there wouldn't be a shirt-tail patch of grass anywhere in the country for foreign stock.

And toward evening two specks of black crawled slowly out of the northwest from Fairhope way, lengthened into freight wagons, and dipped out of sight where the Niobrara River Canyon cut through the tableland. Libby let the thread of her knitting lay in its turns about her finger, the needles rest, and looked after the freight out-fits, knowing how it would be. Sometimes, when there were more important things afoot for those who were the men of the Slogums, she rode a bedroll into town herself, and whipped the tired horses up the long pull from the river crossing to Oxbow Flat.

Often she had seen the heavy wagons creep across Sundance Table, perhaps loaded with stock salt or extended to hold great thirty- or forty-foot ridge logs for sod houses and barns. She had seen the wheels lurch over the edge of the bluffs and slant down toward the river, rolling upon the horses, their collars at their ears, the breeching cutting into their dusty, sweat-streaked thighs, the double-trees pounding their legs as they set themselves against the steep descent amid the jingling of chain harness and the screech of post brakes against the low wheels.

At the easing of the slope the wagons would rumble between dusty clumps of ash and box elder and cottonwood, to plunge their wide-tired wheels into the swift river, churning up the soft, shifting bottom while the men whipped and cursed to keep the horses moving. Then came the long pull out of the Niobrara Canyon, the six- or eight-horse teams straining in the collars, their lathered flanks heaving, the men running alongside with leather-lashed whips, or chunking the wheels at the nearest thing to a level place to give the horses time to blow.

Sometimes the teams were doubled, one wagon resting beside the road, wheels still and tongue down, while another was dragged to the top by the long string of horses pulling with bellies low to the ground, their nostrils flaring. If the horses were balky and there was doubt of their starting again, the pull was made in a straight quarter-mile spurt from the ford to Oxbow Flat under whip and curse, the winded horses floundering desperately for footing in the loose gravel and sand against the drag of the long wagons, the last steep pitch to the top one final plunge under the skinning lashes and the bellowing of the drivers. Then there was the staggering stop of played-out horses and their slow quieting into a long rest before the men had to gather up the lines again for the two miles of flat, rutted road to Slogum House. In the meantime the freighters eased galling collars, rubbed a sagging hip or two with a handful of weeds, or patted a lowered neck. Then, spitting out their tobacco, they drank deeply of the tepid water of a brown jug and wiped their lips on the backs of their sunburned hands. Perhaps someone had a bottle on his hip to kill before Gulla saw it. Empty, the men would consider it mournfully and throw it to the pile of broken glass in a patch of bull-tongue cactus beside the road. Then, replenishing their cuds from the long plugs that wore holes in their back pockets, they would talk about rest and supper and the girls at Slogum House.

Not until the late sun slanted the sparse grass of the hogback to orange was there a moving thing upon the trail that came out of the southwest. Then a faint dot broke from the deepening haze of the horizon. It grew before Libby's eyes, moving swiftly toward Cedar Canyon; horsebackers, she knew, with Winchesters balanced across their saddles, their eyes set upon the heavy wheel tracks leading away from the spot where their new church house had stood the evening before and where perhaps a passer-by to-day had seen only the limestone foundation open to the sky.

They came fast, leaving a wing of dust to spread over the plain as they dipped out of sight into the canyon at the rock crossing. Libby rolled up her knitting and speared it with her needles. Her hand ready on the signal cloth, she watched the men, five of them, ride out upon Oxbow Flat and follow the tracks that led directly to Slogum House.

But as they passed the last fork in the road the horsebackers slowed a little, dropping from a lope to a trot and finally to a walk. At the line fence, a quarter of a mile from Slogum House, they stopped in a semicircle to look toward the end of the hogback that shut out Gulla and her gaunt, wind-blackened sons. A few minutes they see-sawed there. Several times one, probably the tall Pastor Zug himself, started forward and was brought back by the others, until finally they all reined their horses and loped off, but not the way they had come. Instead they took the trail that led down the river to Leo Platt's, riding hard again, passing and repassing each other in their urgency.

Libby looked after them. Some day there would be trouble with Platt, the young locator from the Niobrara who rode openly through the Slogum yard into the Slogum range when it pleased him, his lean hard body a piece with his silver-maned blue roan.

With surveying compass and tripod strapped to his saddle, the man came, teeth white in his wind-browned face, his eyes the bright gray of snow clouds. Gulla watched him from behind the curtain of the shack that was Slogum House then. She looked out upon him with her arms folded over her loose, pudgy stomach and saw that he was an enemy. Yes, there would be trouble with Leo Platt some day. He knew about Gulla's planning in the duskiness of her room, her two dark sons, with their night rides and their hands always over the worn holsters of their guns. Yet he would come, not at the head of five men—fifty perhaps, or alone. Most likely alone.

But the girl's exhilaration lasted no longer than a dry tumbleweed before the flare of a wax match. Wearily she put the surveyor's tall brownness from her as she had often done since the day, five years before, when Gulla caught her running to open the yard gate for him as he came by, opening it and leaning against the gate stick to talk, laughter in her slim young throat and the wind in her silky, smoke-black hair.

With the departure of the five armed men toward Platt's homestead on the Niobrara, Libby's watching for the day was done. Slowly she got up, stretching the stiffness from her body that was long and straight and free of the necessity for the padding and the binding of her sisters, because her excellence, even at twenty-two, was only that of the kitchen.

Whistling the cat to her as one would a dog, Libby strode in her swinging, unmodish step down the path made by the timid feet of her father. The veil, loosed from her face and held only by the hat pins, whipped out far behind her, darkening the green of her long eyes and adding to her air of unconcern something of the aloofness of a thunderhead climbing the summer sky, or the earth under winter snow.

From these things, and because Libby seldom spoke at all, not even to the men who came to eat her food, the others of Slogum House saw indifference to, perhaps even scorn for, their plans and schemes and ambitions. But they needed her and planned never to let her go.

And so, although Gulla knew how things must have been before Libby would leave her place on the ridge, she stood just inside the door looking out upon her coming down the slope of the hogback in the sun of evening, the black tom leaping the soapweeds like a dog, a wild, free dog beside the girl. The mother saw the long, inelegant walk and that the girl's face and bare arms were brown as polished wood from the wind and the sun, and she pulled at her smarting lip angrily. A daughter of Slogum House—fit for nothing but the kitchen.

And out at the barn, Hab, the eldest son of the Slogums, was watching Libby too, the sleep of the day gone from his gaunt, dark face, his hand careless on the forty-four hung over his worn chaps. As the girl neared the house he lifted his drooping black moustache fastidiously from his beaver teeth and spit as a man who must assert himself, spit into the dry horse manure at his feet. Then he wiped his moustache carefully down over his mouth with a red bandanna, his eyes black slits under the brim of his cowman's hat.

At the milk pen, Ward, a long, lanky, tow-haired fourteen-year-old, the youngest son of the Slogums, was driving in the cows. He stopped his pony when he saw Libby coming and waved a hand carelessly high where all might see. His dog Wolf had found a mallard's nest with fourteen eggs and Libby must hear of it.

But when the boy saw Hab watching he whistled to the dog, cracked his quirt at a bulling young heifer, and hurried the milk cows into the hair-clotted barbwire lot.

Apparently seeing none of these things, Libby crossed the yard, her belated chickens running in white waves toward her and breaking before the swirl of her full yellow skirt as she walked straight through the flock. They fell back, clucking a little in bewilderment, and then wandered off toward their roosts. With tail curling, the black cat circled the dejected flock, lifting his deliberate feet high.

Together the two went through the screen door of the side porch into the gloominess that was Slogum House. Across the turn of the hall, pleased so none could come or go without her knowledge, was the door, always ajar, to Gulla's dark room, where she lurked in her crochet slippers.

While the cat settled himself on the high corner shelf in the kitchen to look down upon all its activity, Libby unpinned her veil, folded it into her hat with the ball of knitting from her pocket, and smoothed her hair before the glass in the duskiness of the hall. She ran a comb through it and knotted it again—a simple matter, without the switches, curls, or rolls her mother had bought for her. She did her hair leisurely, despite the awkward rattle of the dishes on the Slogum dining table.

"Babbie!" Gulla commanded impatiently from her room.

Abruptly the sad-footed little thing left her table setting, tripped over a chair, and hurried out with the cob basket. Libby listened to the slam of the screen door. It didn't take Gulla long to train her girls, even simple little Babbie.

As though there were nothing on her mind except supper, Libby went to the kitchen, into the yellow light from the bracket lamp with its fluted tin reflector. She heard no sound behind her, but knew that the thick, squat figure of Gulla in her petticoat and challiesacque was in the shadow of the hall outside the door, her black eyes set low in the bony caverns of her broad face, her lips the dry gray of the lean in salt bacon, her grizzled bangs rolled on tins.

A long time the woman looked in upon this eldest daughter, watching her indolent and yet somehow swift motions as she washed her hands, lifted the lids from the pans and kettles of the supper that was already on, every movement sure as she whirled the flour sieve, tucked the yellow-flaked buttermilk into the biscuits with her finger tips, and turned the light mass out upon the bread board.

"Well?" the mother demanded at last, angry that she could never compel speech from this daughter.

Libby did not look up, just kept turning biscuits in melted butter and placing them in long rows across the black bread pan.

"They came," she said casually, when the pan was finally full.

"Came, came!" the mother exploded. "But how far?"

"To the line fence"—pushing the biscuits into the oven and closing the door swiftly upon the shimmer of heat in her face.

"How many?"

"Five—with Winchesters, I think," taking a malicious satisfaction in this.

"And then—" the mother demanded, tapping her soft slipper in anger.

"Then?—Oh, then? Why, they turned around, just turned around, and rode away again," Libby chanted, making a little song of it as she whipped thick cream into the salad dressing with a fork—not for the freighters, who didn't go for cow feed, as they called it, but for the Slogum table. She said nothing about the men going down to Leo Platt's. And so the mother's face was free to purple at the insolent ditty about rifles and angry men. But the next moment she patted her thick elbows in satisfaction. It was good that they knew where to stop. And some day the line fence would be farther away, much farther away.

NOTE

Mari Sandoz, *Slogum House* (Lincoln: University of Nebraska Press, 1937, 1981); pages selected for inclusion in this volume: chapter 1, 9–20.

5

Mari Sandoz's
Slogum House

Greed as Woman

GLENDA RILEY

In her 1937 novel *Slogum House*, Mari
Sandoz turned the usual stereotype of
greed and cupidity on its head. Instead
of presenting a voracious male rancher
aggrandizing his land holdings to the
detriment of hardworking homesteaders,
Sandoz created Regula Haber Slogum,
a grasping woman who eventually owns
nearly an entire county, which she has
managed to have named after her family.
Although Gulla, as she is known, controls
most of Slogum County, she continues
brutally to foreclose mortgages and force
sheriffs' sales, even during the Depression of the 1930s.[1]

Despite this depiction of what Katharine Mason has called "a
caricature of motherhood," few analysts or critics have analyzed

7. Mari Sandoz, in Estes Park, Colorado, in 1937, finishing *Slogum House*. Helen
Winter Stauffer Collection 200100200314. Mari Sandoz High Plains Heritage
Center.

Sandoz's portrayal of greed as female. Those who have done so have had little to say. Barbara Rippey, in a parenthetical comment, remarked only that a woman who mistreated men and children was "an unlikely thesis" for Sandoz's era. Scott Greenwell hypothesized that Sandoz had made her antagonist female because she realized that "in the animal kingdom the female is frequently the aggressor with an instinct for acquisitiveness."[2]

These superficial probings leave several crucial questions unanswered. Why did Sandoz choose to portray evil as female rather than male? What did Sandoz convey to readers in making her devil a woman? Could a Gulla Slogum have, in fact, existed in the late nineteenth-century and early twentieth-century West?

SLOGUM HOUSE

To answer these questions, one must look first at Sandoz's basic theme. In *Slogum House,* a novel set in two fictitious counties on the Niobrara River in northwestern Nebraska during the 1890s and early 1900s, Sandoz pursued her favorite moral motif—evil (as seen in the corrupt rancher) versus good (as personified by the homesteader). Sandoz's novels, as many commentators have remarked, iterate one complete concern: that the once free and open American West has fallen into the hands of a few selfish and unscrupulous people. In *Slogum House,* Sandoz made it particularly clear that she deplored what she saw as the pillaging of the West—and the "dispossession" of the farmer—by a powerful few.

On the side of evil stand "mortgage holders and landlords," namely Gulla Slogum, who maintains a semblance of womanhood, and her sons, Hab and Cash, whom Gulla uses as her thugs. As *Slogum House* unfolds, the trio build their empire by stealing supplies from hapless settlers and by rustling cattle. Later, they misuse the Homestead and Kinkaid land acts, which Sandoz believed to be "the hope of the poor man." The unscrupulous Slogums file on plots of land in the name of each family member and even of hired helpers at Slogum House.[3]

Representing the presence of good is Gulla's amiable but ineffective husband, Ruedy, whom Gulla has tricked into marrying her. Although Gulla had hoped to gain position and wealth by marrying into Ruedy's family, its members have shunned her, and Gulla determines to outdo them. Along with two of Gulla's and Ruedy's children, Libby and Ward, Ruedy symbolizes kindness. Neither he nor the children has the fortitude to interfere with and halt Gulla's nefarious plans, yet they refuse to act as her pawns.

Because Gulla, Hab, and Cash represent immorality while Ruedy, Libby, and Ward epitomize virtue, the Slogum family stands divided, but Gulla tips the balance in her direction by subverting two more children to her purposes. She goads her twin daughters, Annette and Cellie, to prostitute themselves to local officials, notably the sheriff and judge, to protect Hab and Cash from prosecution and to pick up any information that might hint of legal trouble for the Slogums.

Gulla also keeps several upstairs "girls" as prostitutes for the cowboys and freighters who board at the roadhouse called Slogum House. Late each evening, Gulla skulks through a specially built passageway so she can monitor the conversations of family members and freighters alike, gleaning information useful in her rise to power.

Gulla and Slogum House earn disrepute throughout the Sandhills region, yet no one seems able to stop Gulla Slogum. For example, she frees Hab and Cash of a murder conviction by ordering the slaying of a key witness. She eliminates others who oppose her and hires shady lawyers to pursue her causes. Whenever Gulla's own children resist her edicts, she backs them down. When Cash stands up to her, Gulla intimidates him with a bald show of authority mixed with intimidation. She insults him, seizes his rifle and empties it of shells, and threatens to reveal his deeds to the sheriff. After Libby runs away from Slogum House, Gulla fetches her back. When Ward courts a Polish girl, Gulla tells falsehoods that turn the Polish community against Ward. She seems unconcerned when a group of Polish men attack him and maim him for life. And the night Annette tries to run off with her lover, René, Gulla arranges for Hab and others to beat him.

Throughout these events, Ruedy remains miserable, yet acquiescent in his wife's schemes. Increasingly, he works his own sparse claim and lives in a soddy he has built there. Only when he learns that René has been castrated does Ruedy lash back, killing the castrator, skinning the man's horse, tanning the hide to use as a rug before his own fireplace. Ruedy keeps his deeds secret, however, and fails to confront Gulla.

The outcome of this morality play is much what one would expect. The evil players pay for their sins. Gulla, Hab, and Cash are unable to enjoy what they have acquired, continuing to intimidate and steal long after their corrals overflow with cattle. For Gulla, punishment comes in the form of a lingering death, caught in her own massive flesh and dependent, at last, on Ruedy and Libby. For Hab and Cash, death comes swiftly yet horribly.

Sandoz rewards the forces of morality. Sandoz explained that because she would never emphasize "hopelessness of the struggle in the sandhills," in *Slogum House* "the meek do inherit the earth."[4] Ruedy prospers and builds a larger home, where he lodges family members as they desert Gulla. He also turns his blooming claim into a sanctuary for the very people whom Gulla has driven off their land.

In addition, the "good" Slogum children achieve their own sorts of victory. Libby finally flees Slogum House and takes refuge in Ruedy's calm valley. She remains strong and stable, a fine woman of good character. Ward eventually dies of his beating yet attains glory in death. Because he had helped poor homesteaders, Ward's funeral draws everyone in the area—except Gulla, his own mother.

Still, in a sense, Gulla is the victor. Her greed has dried up the Sandhills for everyone but the Slogums. She has disabled her children and made them unproductive, for not one of them marries and has children. Her three sons eventually die. Of her daughters,

Libby remains alienated from the man she loves, Annette becomes a religious fanatic, and Cellie withers into an aging, faded shell of herself. Gulla's children are as incapable of happiness and peopling the land as the homesteaders.[5]

RESPONSE TO SLOGUM HOUSE

Of course, when *Slogum House* first appeared in 1937 it spoke to a generation of poverty-stricken Americans, battered by the worst depression in the nation's history. Numerous farmers especially begged the U.S. Congress and state legislatures for emergency aid. Sandoz herself had watched as more than four thousand farmers silently marched in Lincoln, Nebraska, pleading for state assistance.[6] Many such farmers, as well as numerous factory workers, blamed powerful financiers for their misery. Because *Slogum House* analyzed financial disasters and indicted the acquisitive and corrupt Gulla, Sandoz became the voice of numerous Americans. Her publishers reprinted *Slogum House* twice in November and again in December.[7]

Slogum House received enough favorable reviews that Sandoz termed the critics "very grand," dismissing those who were less approving. She said that Clifton Fadiman's dislike of her work constituted "rank flattery," while she diffused Howard Mumford Jones's comments that the book proved "fatiguing" and full of "artistic monotony" by referring to him as Mummy Jones.[8]

Other criticism was more difficult to scorn. Eastern readers failed to embrace *Slogum House*, apparently because they objected to Sandoz's blaming eastern capitalists and entrepreneurs for the West's predicament. Sandoz made no secret of her belief that the "entrenched East" had treated the West as a colony to be exploited by financiers and speculators.[9] Before publication, Sandoz's editor had tried to soften her anti-eastern theme, but to no avail. Sandoz had replied: "I realize you are looking out for your eastern readers and the critics. . . . I don't give a good goddam about the whole raft of readers and critics. . . . I'm in the writing business for the writing and the rest is certainly very incidental."[10] It was one thing to talk about writing for writing's sake, but when fewer readers purchased *Slogum House* than Sandoz had hoped, she was forced to take notice. Besides resenting Sandoz's anti-eastern bias, readers took umbrage at her dark view of the West and the novel's explicit language and lurid situations. One reviewer suggested that many readers would see *Slogum House* as "sordid and obscene" although it was "free of any gratuitous intention in these respects." Another judged that it was "written with power" yet "overburdened with violence to a point that occasionally touches burlesque."[11]

Readers themselves wrote to Sandoz, some pouring out their disappointment or chagrin. To one of these, Sandoz replied that a person might dislike *Slogum House* and still "see its serious purpose," adding that she would not waste her time on anything without a larger purpose.[12] Some libraries and bookstores, especially in Sandoz's home state of Nebraska, boycotted *Slogum House*, presumably objecting to Sandoz's representation of Nebraska to the rest of the nation—the reviewer for *Time* had referred to the Nebraska Sandhills as a "wild environment." Early in 1938, Omaha mayor Dan E. Butler banned *Slogum House* from Omaha public libraries. The McCook County Public Library placed *Slogum House* on its "rotten row" of books judged objectionable because of their language or slurs upon groups.[13]

This mixed reception discouraged Sandoz, who had hoped for more comprehension from the reading public. She may have had difficulty communicating her ideas because she had configured *Slogum House* as an allegory. She had recently discovered Friedrich Nietzsche's theory of the will-to-power individual and had decided to present her social criticism through one person, Gulla Slogum, and one situation, Slogum House.[14] Complicating the allegory further, Sandoz characterized northwestern Nebraska as symbolic of the entire nation, which "was so short a time ago the land of promise." In Sandoz's view, the country now lay "paralyzed, all activity halted except foreclosure and eviction and the lengthening lines of those who had no roof and no bread." To reinforce her point, Sandoz invoked the words of Jeremiah: "And I brought you into a plentiful country, to eat the fruit thereof and the goodness thereof: but when ye entered, ye defiled my land, and made mine heritage an abomination."

Sandoz was disappointed that most readers missed the allegory. It seems easily understandable that someone like Sandoz, from a struggling homestead family in western Nebraska, would raise questions about the plight of farm families living in the once golden West, but her analysis seemed to go over most readers' heads. According to Sandoz, "it seemed over-obvious when I planned it, yet only a lawyer or two got the idea."[15]

Not only did Sandoz baffle her readers with allegory, but she also confused them by choosing a woman, Gulla Slogum, as the symbol of greed. During the 1930s, most Americans continued to idealize women as mothers, keepers of home and families, and inculcators of virtue and morality. To many, a Gulla Slogum would have been incomprehensible and inconceivable.

WOMEN IN THE DEPRESSION

In addition to Americans' long-standing propensity to romanticize women, the Depression years largely cast women as sympathetic figures, unfortunate victims of hard times. Although working women often supported themselves and their children, or helped support their families, they were fired at a terrifying rate. Three out of ten white women workers lost their jobs, while more than half of African American women workers did so. Those who continued to work held low-status, often menial positions that paid on average only half of what men earned, $525 compared to $1,027 for men per year.[16]

Married women lost their jobs at an even greater rate than single women. Because many Americans still believed that women worked primarily for "pin money" rather than to support themselves, they argued that all available jobs should go to men. When the Economy Act of 1933 prohibited two members of the same family from holding positions with the federal government, such groups as the League of Women Voters and the National Women's Party protested, but a significant number of workers, three-fourths of them women, had to leave their jobs. State and local governments soon instituted similar policies.[17]

Women professionals lost their jobs as well. Three out of four school boards refused to hire married women and the percentage of female teachers dropped from 81 percent to 75.7 percent by the end of the decade. In professions as a whole, the number of women fell from 14.2 percent in 1930 to 12.3 percent by 1940. Accordingly, women's college enrollment dropped from 43.7 percent in 1930 to 40.2 in 1940.[18]

The prototype for the powerful, grasping Gulla Slogum was someone other than the average American woman. Those few Depression-era women who did occupy positions of authority were usually admirable. Rather than amassing resources and authority for themselves, as did the corrupt and voracious Gulla, they devoted their energies to helping the distressed nation. Among these women were First Lady Eleanor Roosevelt, Secretary of Labor Frances Perkins, Director of the Division of Negro Affairs of the National Youth Administration Mary McLeod Bethune, head of women's and professional projects for the Works Progress Administration Ellen Sullivan Woodward, and a horde of social workers called to Washington as members of President Franklin Delano Roosevelt's New Deal programs. On the level of the common folk were such labor leaders as Ella Reeves "Mother" Bloor, Luisa Moreno, Emma Tenayuca, and Meridel LeSueur.[19]

Of course, one might argue that Depression-era Americans feared women's increasing power, and Gulla may have been an indictment of such might. Depression-era women did exercise some leverage. Many supported their families because they could get part-time, menial labor while their husbands could get nothing.

Eleanor Roosevelt was the first politically active First Lady; Frances Perkins the first female cabinet member; Nellie Taylor Ross the first female director of the mint; and Ruth Bryan Owen, minister to Denmark, the first woman ambassador. Among American laborers, women of all races, especially Latinas, served as union activists and strikers.[20]

Still, it would be difficult to construe Sandoz's theme into a warning about women's inability to manage increasing power. The women mentioned above were not only effective at their jobs, but they refused to use them to enlarge their authority or causes. Frances Perkins avoided utilizing her position to further feminist agendas, while Mary McLeod Bethune seldom used her considerable influence to challenge the existing policy of segregation.[21]

On Sandoz's Great Plains lived thousands of poverty-stricken, despairing women. Certainly, the national image of rural women was Dorothea Lange's touching photograph *The Migrant Mother* (1936). There was also a fair share of female government officials, lawyers, reformers, writers, and social critics such as Sandoz herself. Other women fought the effects of the Depression through union activism. During the 1930s, Manuela Solis Sager organized garment and agricultural workers in Texas and in 1935 helped form the Texas Agricultural Workers' Union. Sager also collaborated with San Antonio organizers, notably Emma Tenayuca, who played a crucial role in the Pecan Shellers Strike of 1938.[22]

Fear of women's changing roles did, however, show itself in insidious ways, especially in the market and media. For example, the 1930 Sears Roebuck catalogue, widely read and utilized in the West, frequently reminded women to remain "feminine." Its illustrated advertisements emphasized long, flowing skirts and dresses, indented waistlines, molded bustlines, and corsets. In media, motion pictures spread a similar message. Jean Harlow bleached her hair and became the screen's first blond seductress. Marlene Dietrich, Bette Davis, Greta Garbo, and Mae West paraded women's sensuality with their "bedroom eyes" and painted lips.[23]

Advisers and teachers also warned women to remember that they bore special responsibilities to American civilization. Etiquettes and guidebooks focused on the need for women to maintain moral standards, especially now that automobiles carried dating couples away from home and provided mobile bedrooms. Meanwhile, the marriage-and-family courses rife in high schools, colleges, and universities, advocated marriage and motherhood for the nation's women.[24]

None of the women leaders resembled Sandoz's Gulla Slogum in acquisitiveness or selfishness, and while the movie vamps and the emphasis on training girls to be ladylike showed some unease, nothing like Gulla Slogum was apparent in American life, media, politics, or film, either nationally or on the plains. From where, then, did Gulla Slogum come?

Claire Mattern has suggested that Sandoz's hostility toward her mother, Mary, led her to portray Mary as Gulla and herself as the independent Libby, who was even an accurate shot and frequent hunter like Mari. The opposition of Gulla (Mary) and Libby (Mari) thus played out the mother-daughter struggle that had shadowed Mari Sandoz's life.[25] It is true that in 1933 Sandoz had written harshly of her mother, who had opposed her career as an author. She added that "there's no discounting the antagonism the average woman feels for the eldest daughter."[26] But by the time Sandoz wrote *Slogum House*, she had largely reconciled with her mother and dissipated a great deal of her hostility toward both her parents in *Old Jules*, which had appeared in 1935.[27]

IMAGES OF WOMEN IN THE WEST

Other explanations of Sandoz's decision to portray greed as woman are more likely. Sandoz, a westerner herself, was realistic about myths of the American West. Seeing both the bright and dark sides of the region and its peoples, she frequently tried to dispel mythology, as evidenced in her debunking of Buffalo Bill Cody. Sandoz not only set out to reveal the chaos in the American West but also to show

how adherence to myths of the West and its inhabitants could blind people and keep them from action.[28]

For another thing, Sandoz demonstrated a long-standing interest in western women, by which she meant female Anglo settlers. Although Sandoz later wrote several books concerning American Indians, she had little to say specifically about Native women.[29] Nor did Sandoz write about other women of color, although her biographer, Helen Winter Stauffer, pointed out that Sandoz came to see herself as a writer interested in "destruction of discrimination between economic levels, between nationalist levels, between color levels and so on."[30]

In describing western women, Sandoz, like most writers of her time, focused upon white female migrants. Unlike most authors of the era, however, Sandoz observed the entire spectrum from drudges to professional women. While historians Emerson Hough and Everett Dick presented women in highly stereotypical terms as the salvation of the frontier, and writer Hamlin Garland often characterized them as broken in body and spirit, Sandoz took an even-handed view.[31]

Because Sandoz could see the problematic features of the West and its myth, she could also see the dark side of western women and their images. Some were staunch pioneer mothers while others gave in to a variety of pressures. In Sandoz's *Old Jules*, for example, some women crumbled, but others persisted. Henriette, Jules's second wife, asserted herself by pursuing a career as postmistress and eventually divorcing Jules. In addition, a Mrs. Surber guarded her daughters against early marriage and urged them toward careers. Twenty years after *Old Jules*, in 1955, Sandoz restored a long-overlooked group—women frontier doctors—to the limelight when she depicted Dr. Morissa Kirk in *Miss Morissa*.[32]

Sandoz clearly believed that western women could be good or evil, weak or strong, submissive or aggressive. She noted that "the many women" among Nebraska settlers often vied with their menfolk for the role of boss, and some "plainly ran things." Sandoz also found women resilient: "nor were the women, bossy or not, always easy to drive out. Some clung to the homestead even after their husbands were shot down by ranch-hirelings." Thus, in her view, western women could be civilizers who also added "gaiety" to the scene or could be forces of destruction, greed, and despair.[33]

Sandoz did not automatically impute evil to one gender or the other. "I cannot think of people as divided into sexes," she wrote, "so much as into types. To me there are only people, varying a great deal among themselves." She added that "because I think men with dictator complexes are not sufficiently male, I made my will-to-power individual an ambitious woman."[34]

In choosing to liken greed and woman, Sandoz imparted— purposefully or not—certain messages to her audience. Gulla defied every western convention of the times—and, in doing so, probably further perplexed a goodly number of readers. For instance, many Americans thought of the West as female, a ripe, fertile source of abundance often defiled by rapacious men. Sandoz's Gulla ran counter to this image. Not only did men defile the West, but women pillaged it as well. And what of the widespread belief that women settlers civilized the West, making it good, kind, and gentle for all those who came after them? Sandoz presented "bad" women who cheated, lied, and prostituted themselves to amass wealth and influence. If women weren't the force carrying virtue to the West, what was? How would readers react to the concept that greed was not equated with gender? Even into the beginning of the twenty-first century, many Americans continue to believe that women are gentle and giving, while men are rough and selfish.

And what about *Slogum House* as metaphor for home? Americans usually thought of the home as a female preserve, a calm, virtuous, refuge, yet Gulla had turned her family's home, Slogum House, into a nest of voracity, power, corruption. The implications of Sandoz's ideas—whether she intended them or not—were that women, home, and family were not necessarily pure and sacrosanct. In *Slogum House* everything was corruptible: women, home, family, farm, the West, and, through allegory, the United States itself.[35] Even if Sandoz did not plan it, the ramifications were staggering; *Slogum House* forced readers to question the validity of their beliefs regarding a large number of their most sacred institutions.

Such personal inquiry was all the more frightening in 1937 because the West obviously *had* sunk to a low point. Millions of Americans would have agreed with Sandoz that the West appeared increasingly bankrupt. A combination of overcultivation and drought had made such states as Kansas, Oklahoma, and Texas vulnerable to ravaging winds that stripped the soil and left a Dust Bowl. Despite relative prosperity in the Southwest and the Pacific Northwest, tragedy after tragedy raked the plains. As a result, thousands abandoned worn-out fields, while western states applied for one federal subsidy after another.

MODELS FOR WICKED WOMEN

Despite all this, however, *Slogum House* would have lacked impact if, in fact, a Gulla Slogum could not have lived and breathed in the American West. Thus, the critical question is: could there have been a Gulla? Did women and situations like those Sandoz described exist?

The answer to these questions is an unqualified yes. Sandoz was far too diligent a historian to create a false character. She had spent twenty years taking notes for *Slogum House,* and a family who appeared in *Old Jules* clearly provided the prototype for the Slogums. Mollie Schwartz not only ran a roadhouse, but her sons acquired supplies through nighttime raids and her two daughters prostituted themselves with local officials.[36]

People all over the West wrote to Sandoz, claiming they personally knew the woman who had served as Gulla's model. According to them, she lived in a neighboring town or in the next county.[37] Six years after *Slogum House,* Minnesota/Manitoba writer Martha Ostenso published *O River Remember,* a novel that also portrays a tyrannical matriarch whose greed blights her family and community. It is, of course, possible that Ostenso was familiar with *Slogum*

House, at any rate she thought this kind of character plausible. Like Sandoz, Ostenso had grown up on a homestead frontier, and her first book, *Wild Geese* (1925), portrays a tyrannical patriarch not entirely unlike *Old Jules*.[38] Despite contemporary idealizations of women, many North Americans knew an individual woman or two who failed to fit the romanticized mode.

Historians of western women have indicated that Sandoz's female antagonist and specific situations were common. For instance, in *Slogum House* Gulla trapped Ruedy because she was pregnant, a circumstance she blamed on him. Even though popular culture deified female settlers as highly virtuous civilizers and helpmates, thousands of them "fell by the way," as a German woman of the 1870s phrased it. "Rush" marriages were far from uncommon and paternity suits appeared in the courts. In 1881 the defendant—an unwed mother—in *Caverly v. Canfield* charged seduction, in that she had no prior knowledge of sex and had been drugged. Popular westerns like Zane Grey novels also contained subplots of girls seduced and abandoned, only to be vindicated in the end. It is conceivable that Gulla became pregnant and the seemingly weak-willed Ruedy succumbed to her accusation rather than challenge it.[39]

In *Slogum House* Gulla also created a troubled marriage and a dysfunctional family, hardly *Little House on the Prairie*. In truth, however, dysfunction could, and did, occur with bewildering frequency. The rising divorce rate during the late nineteenth century distressed many Americans, who became even more troubled in 1908 when Commissioner of Labor Carroll D. Wright reported that "the divorce rate increases as one goes westward."[40]

Everything from divorce records to novels reveals that many western divorces resulted from verbal and physical abuse, some as heinous as Gulla's.[41] For a range of complicated reasons, the accused abusers were usually male, but even during the Victorian hearts-and-romance 1880s and 1890s, some women abused family members. For instance, J. Dayton Thorpe testified before an Oklahoma territorial court in 1895 that his wife, Abbie, had struck and beat him on more than one hundred occasions, had pointed a revolver at him, which she repeatedly snapped to intimidate him, and had thrown a pair of scissors at him. Thorpe added that Abbie had regularly called him a "damned old fool" and a "damn son-of-a-bitch" and had told him to "go to hell" although he had asked her "civil questions." According to Thorpe, Abbie had eventually abandoned him and their daughter, saying "she did not want the child that it looked too much like its father, she had no use for it."[42] If Thorpe's testimony was accurate, Abbie developed some ploys that Gulla Slogum might have found useful.

Besides helping create a miserable home life and mistreating family members, Gulla Slogum was also responsible for hiding outlaws from the sheriff and for rustling cattle. Could a woman combining *all* these deviant behaviors have existed in the American West? The case of Belle Starr suggests that, again, the answer is yes.[43]

Belle Starr was involved in at least two marriages, both highly dysfunctional, and she cohabited with other men of questionable reputation. Also, like Gulla, Belle controlled her daughter for her own purposes. In 1880, when Belle—then known as Myra Maybelle Reed—married Sam Starr, she took the name Belle. She also changed her eleven-year-old daughter's name, Rosie Lee, to Pearl. Belle had been training Pearl for the stage, but Pearl developed incapacitating dizzy spells. Thus, Belle decided that Pearl—like Gulla's daughter Fanny—would be a "lady" who would represent the family favorably.[44]

Because Belle intended Pearl to help the family by marrying a man of substance, she refused to let Pearl wed the man she loved. When Pearl became pregnant by her sweetheart, Belle advocated abortion and banished the girl when she refused to comply. Pearl took refuge with her grandmother and gave birth but eventually agreed to return to Belle without the child. After that, mother and daughter attended dances, rode in public, and appeared at other public functions together (220–29).

If Belle Starr's public appearances with Pearl resembled Gulla's with Annette and Cellie, the two women are also similar in their private harboring of outlaws. While not as notorious on this score as legends suggest, Starr admitted that "boys who were friends of mine," including the notorious Jesse James, "visited" her for weeks at a time (147–48). Even Starr's primary biographer, Glenn Shirley—who, like Belle, belonged to the Shirley family and was determined to dispel myths—noted that there was "some basis in fact" for the many stories about Belle hiding outlaws in Robbers Cave (151). Shirley added that other wanted men sought refuge with Belle and Sam Starr. In 1884 John Middleton, who had a price on his head for murder, came to Belle, who probably took him in (177–85). The following year, local authorities, who found several outlaws in the Starr home, accused Belle of being a "gang" leader. As was the case with Gulla Slogum, the charges failed to stick when witnesses proved either vague or absent, and the court released Belle (188–202).

Like Gulla Slogum, Belle Starr was a rustler of sorts. In 1882 she was charged with horse stealing in Fort Smith, Arkansas. In this, her first arrest and hearing, Belle—like Gulla—took charge. She guided the defense by sending frequent notes to her attorneys, who reportedly paid close attention to her missives. In addition, one of the key witnesses fled to Texas and was never heard of again. Still, the court convicted Belle and sentenced her to two consecutive six-month terms in a workhouse (151–65).

In 1886 a Fort Smith court issued a writ for Belle's arrest for stealing a mare. She turned herself in and put up the required bond, claiming she was innocent. After hearing conflicting evidence, a court eventually released her (188–202). A scant two years later, a rancher named Hi Early complained that Belle had run off his horses and cattle. Belle confronted Early on a trail, firing her gun past his head and threatening to kill him if he made any more charges. Undaunted, Early offered a seventy-five-dollar reward to anyone who would kill Belle Starr (246–47).

Like Gulla, Belle emulated ladylike demeanor, presumably to improve her image. Gulla used corsets and styled hair, as well as plucking her facial hair, and Belle wore long skirts, gold earrings, and hats with feathers and rode sidesaddle. When traveling alone, Belle wore a Colt .45, which she called "my baby" (171–73). On occasion, she shot at a man to make him pick up her hat or get out of her way or demonstrate whatever action she thought was her due as a lady. She also frequented Fort Smith saloons, where she played the piano and gambled for high stakes, yet refused to smoke cigars because it was unladylike (194–97).

Despite her affectations of civilized behavior, Belle Starr, like Gulla, eventually fell victim to her own greed and meanness. To improve her lands, which she held under questionable title, Belle exploited sharecroppers. In 1889 someone shot her dead, and a sharecropper with whom she had had a dispute was charged. He was never convicted, but officials gave up the search for Belle's assassin (230–45).

It appears that Gulla Slogum surpassed Belle Starr in only one way: Gulla kept "upstairs girls" as prostitutes and even prodded her daughters to exchange their bodies for goods and favors. Gulla's behavior, however, was not altogether unusual. Prostitutes and madams of all races, creeds, and ethnic backgrounds abounded throughout the West, not only in mining camps, cattle towns, and near military forts, but in such agricultural centers as Grand Island, Nebraska, and among such pious groups as Utah Mormons.[45] It would not take long for someone as ambitious as Gulla to recognize that providing sexual services to western men would turn a fair profit.

Gulla was only one of numerous western mothers who condoned or even initiated their daughters' profession. Some mothers worked side by side with their daughters. According to historian Anne M. Butler, "The presence of children, often fully involved in the mother's occupation, manifested itself as a common frontier occurrence."[46] Motherhood did not necessarily deter women from prostituting their own daughters. Butler observed that "some young women came to prostitution . . . as the result of deliberate actions by the mother." In 1875, for example, the owner of a Denver cigar store provided her twelve-year-old daughter as a prostitute for customers and later added another twelve-year-old girl to her offerings.[47]

Even Belle Starr's daughter, Pearl, ultimately blamed her mother for her own entry into prostitution. Shortly after Belle's death, Pearl married and divorced, then took up residence in a brothel at Fort Smith. She soon opened her own "boardinghouse," which boasted a string of pearls and electric lights across its front, defending her choice of profession by saying everyone knew "the conditions" under which she had lived.[48]

GREED AS WOMAN

It appears, then, that Gulla Slogum was a true-to-life figure, genuine in her machinations and transgressions. Sandoz offered her readers a reprieve from Gulla and her avarice by allowing Gulla to triumph only in the amassing of her fortune. Gulla was never able to take pleasure in her wealth or her family; she had no grandchildren to sustain her in old age. And, perhaps most significantly of all, Gulla never returned to Ohio to best the Slogums who had once shunned her. On the other hand, greed will not necessarily die with Gulla. Sandoz does not indicate who will inherit Gulla's vast holdings. The optimistic reader might conclude that at least a portion of Gulla's land will revert to Ruedy, who would use it wisely and well, but, with her sons dead, most of Gulla's landed empire is likely to fall into the hands of one of her daughters. Perhaps Fanny, absent throughout much of the novel, will rise in Gulla's place and become another base, will-to-power person.

Clearly, Gulla Slogum is forceful and even frightening. Sandoz had observed widely and well, recognizing that people could be good or evil despite their gender. In the same way that Sandoz saw the negative aspects of the American West, which had turned from a dream to a nightmare in her own day, she could perceive the contrary side of women. By presenting woman as greed, Sandoz may have offended or confused conventionally minded readers, but greed as woman probably proved more effective in shaking people's beliefs than yet another covetous male rancher or entrepreneur would have done. Although most readers missed Sandoz's allegory, they could not escape its impact.

NOTES

The author would like to thank John Wunder at the University of Nebraska–Lincoln for his extremely helpful suggestions and Donald E. Green at Chadron State College for the opportunity to present a version of this paper to the 1995 annual meeting of the Mari Sandoz Society.

1. Sandoz, *Slogum House.*
2. Mason, "Greed and the Erosion of the Pioneer Ethic"; Rippey, "Mari Sandoz' Historical Perspective," 63; Greenwell, "Fascists in Fiction," 136.
3. Quoted in Sandoz, *Old Jules Country,* 288.
4. Sandoz to editorial offices of Longman, Green & Co., New York, December 2, 1933, University of Nebraska–Lincoln, Mari Sandoz Archives (hereafter called UNL Archives).
5. Stauffer, *Mari Sandoz* (1982), 37.
6. Stauffer, *Mari Sandoz,* 126.
7. Sandoz, *Slogum House,* printing history on copyright page.
8. Sandoz to Paul Hoffman, December 15, 1937, UNL Archives; Howard Mumford Jones, review of *Slogum House, Saturday Review of Literature* 17 (November 27, 1937): 6 and Sandoz to J. R. de la Torre Bueno Jr., September 16, 1942, UNL Archives.
9. Stauffer, *Mari Sandoz* (1982), 116–17, and Stauffer, *Mari Sandoz* (1987), 18. See also Sandoz to Alfred R. McIntyre, March 22, 1937, UNL Archives.
10. Sandoz to Edward Weeks, September 19, 1936, UNL Archives.
11. Margaret Wallace, review of *Slogum House, New York Times,* November 28, 1937, sec, 7, p. 6, and unsigned review of *Slogum House, Time* 30 (November 29, 1937): 69.
12. Sandoz to Jeannette N. Shefferd, February 25, 1938, UNL Archives.
13. Margaret Wallace's review of *Slogum House* in *Time* 30 (November 29, 1937): 69; *Omaha World-Herald,* January 17 and 18, 1937.
14. Mattern, "Mari Sandoz: Her Use of Allegory in *Slogum House,*" 119–281; Stauffer, "Mari Sandoz" in *Literary History of the American West,* 770; and Stauffer, *Mari Sandoz* (1982), 37. See also Nietzsche, *Will to Power,* and Mencken, *Philosophy of Friedrich Nietzsche.*

15. Sandoz to Russell Gibbs, March 30, 1939, UNL Archives.

16. Riley, *Inventing the American Woman*, 256; See also Blackwelder, "Women in the Work Force."

17. Helpful studies are Lois Scharf, *To Work and to Wed*, and Eileen Boris, "Regulating Industrial Homework."

18. Riley, *Inventing the American Woman*, 258.

19. For Eleanor Roosevelt, see Beasley, *Eleanor Roosevelt and the Media*; Cook, *Eleanor Roosevelt 1844–*; Scharf, *Eleanor Roosevelt: The First Lady of American*; and Youngs, *Eleanor Roosevelt: A Personal and Public Life*. For other New Deal women, see Patterson, "Mary Dewson and the American Minimum Wage Movement," and Martha H. Swain, "Forgotten Woman." For labor leaders, see Blackwelder, *Women of the Depression*; Duron, "Mexican Women and Labor Conflict in Los Angeles"; and Wortman, "Gender Issues in the National Farmers Union in the 1930s."

20. Riley, *Inventing the American Woman*, 259, 263.

21. See Smith, "Mary McLeod Bethune," 113–27.

22. Schwieder and Fink, "Plains Women"; and Westin, *Making Do*.

23. See, for example, Honey, "Images of Women in *The Saturday Evening Post*, 1931–36"; Sochen, "Mildred Pierce and Women in Film" and *Mae West*; and Bergman, *We're in the Money*.

24. Bailey, "Scientific Truth . . . and Love."

25. Mattern, "Mari Sandoz," 135–37. For a discussion of Sandoz's relationships to her mother, see also Graulich, "Every Husband's Right."

26. Sandoz to Tyler Bucheneau, December 6, 1933, UNL Archives.

27. Mattern, "Rebels, Aliens, Outsiders," and Yuvajita, "Changing Images of Women," 200–205.

28. Stauffer, *Mari Sandoz* (1982), 3–4.

29. Powell, "Bearer of Beauty."

30. Quoted in Stauffer, *Mari Sandoz* (1982), 5–6.

31. Hough, *Passing of the Frontier*; Dick, *Sod-House Frontier* and "Sunbonnet and Calico"; and Garland, *Pioneer Mother*. For changing ideas regarding western women's images—and an understanding of how long it took for those images to approach reality—see Larson, "Dolls, Vassals, and Drudges," and "Women's Role in the West"; Riley, "Images of the Frontierswoman"; Stoeltje, "'A Helpmate for Man Indeed'"; Armitage, "Western Women"; E. Jameson, "Women as Workers, Women as Civilizers"; Underwood, "Western Women and True Womanhood"; Oshana, "Native American Women in

Westerns"; Riley, "Continuity and Change"; and Castaneda, "Women of Color and the Rewriting of Western History."

32. Yuvajita, "Changing Images of Women," 179–93, 207–9, and Limbaugh, "Feminist Reads Old Jules." That such women doctors existed on the Great Plains is indicated in Fride Van Dalsem and Abbie Jarvis, Pioneer Daughters Collection, South Dakota State Historical Research Center; Laughlin, "Dr. Georgia Arbuckle Fix," 188–89; and Rowland, *As Long as Life*.

33. Quoted in Sandoz, *Old Jules Country*, 292–93, 300. See also Yuvajita, "Changing Images of Women," 223, 229.

34. Sandoz to Beatrice Blackmar Gould, March 23, 1938, and to F. B. Griffith, January 7, 1941, UNL Archives.

35. Rippey, "Mari Sandoz' Historical Perspective," 60–68.

36. Sandoz to Cassandra L. Bloom, February 28, 1938, UNL Archives; and Whitaker, "Violence in *Old Jules* and *Slogum House*," 223.

37. Stauffer, *Mari Sandoz* (1982), 38; and Sandoz to Judge Louis Lightner, March 3, 1938, UNL Archives.

38. Ostenso, *O River Remember* and *Wild Geese*.

39. Louise Sophia Gellhorn Boylan, "My Life Story: Reminiscences of German Settlers in Hardin County, 1867–1883," Iowa State Historical Society, Iowa City. The court case is found in James S. Ewing, Short Addresses, n.d., 93–133, McLean County Historical Society, Bloomington IL. Also helpful is Joan M. Jensen, "Death of Rosa."

40. Quoted in Riley, *Divorce*, 86. See also Robert L. Griswold, "Apart But Not Adrift,"265–84 and *Family and Divorce in California*; Petrik, "If She Be Content"; and Riley, "Torn Asunder."

41. Graulich, "Violence Against Women"; Gonda, "Not a Matter of Choice"; and Downey, "Battered Pioneers." Also helpful in understanding this phenomenon are Schlissel, "Frontier Families," and Richard Griswold del Castillo, *La Familia*.

42. Case #1978, Thorpe v. Thorpe, filed July 25, 1895, Territorial Records, Logan County. Similar findings in California cases between 1850 and 1890 are reported in Robert Griswold, *Family and Divorce in California*, 1–17, 120–40, 170–79.

43. Some recent nonfiction treatments of Belle Starr include Glenn Shirley, *Outlaw Queen*; Hicks, *Belle Starr and Her Pearl*; Hardcastle, *Legend of Belle Starr*; Winn, *Two Starrs*; Edson, *Wanted Belle Starr*; Betty M. Shirley, *Belle Starr and Her Roots*; Stanley, *Belle Starr's Life and Hard Times*; Steele, *Starr Tracks*; Glenn Shirley, *Belle Starr and Her*; and Green, *Belle Starr*.

44. Glenn Shirley, *Belle Starr and Her Times*, 144. All further citations to Belle Starr are from this source and are given in parentheses in the text.

45. Hirata, "Free, Indentured, Enslaved"; Butler, "Military Myopia"; McCormick, "Red Lights in Zion"; Diffendal, "Prostitution in Grand Island, Nebraska"; Petrik, "Prostitution in Helena, Montana"; Murphy, "Private Lives of Public Women"; Butler, *Daughters of Joy*; Wegars, "'Inmates of Body Houses'"; and Tong, *Unsubmissive Women*.

46. Butler, *Daughters of Joy*, 35.

47. Butler, *Daughters of Joy*, 41.

48. Glenn Shirley, *Belle Starr and Her Times*, 252–54.

8. Sioux camp, east of Chadron, Nebraska. Ernest Slattery Collection 200300200006. Mari Sandoz High Plains Heritage Center.

During the late 1940s, the U.S. government instituted a program of "termination and relocation," Indian policy designed to end federal responsibilities to American Indian tribes. The policy, intended to terminate tribal reservations and tribes and to relocate Indians into mainstream American society, had devastating consequences. Many Native people ended up starving and destitute in cities, or penniless and adrift in what had been their homeland. To bring the plight of Native people to the reading public and give a sense of the dignity and honor of the people she counted as friends, Sandoz published several versions of her article "What the Indians Taught Me" in popular national magazines and in book form as *These Were the Sioux* (1961). She saw the importance of including women's stories and voices in all of her work, and in these writings, readers learned about Sioux women at a time when the only people more invisible than American Indians were American Indian women. In her essay, Shannon Smith points out that Sandoz was a harbinger of ethnohistorical techniques, as she wrote about American Indians, and a forerunner for including Indian women in her stories of the West.

6

Excerpt from "What the Sioux Taught Me"

MARI SANDOZ

When I read stories of crime and violence in the newspapers I think of the old buffalo-hunting Sioux and Cheyenne Indians and their training of the young. The American Indian as I knew him had much to teach us about rearing children to live free, useful, well-adjusted lives.

I grew up near the Sioux reservation at Pine Ridge, S.D. My father and mother were busy with the land. As the oldest of six children, the care of the youngsters fell to me.

One morning the summer I was eight a playmate from an Indian camp across the road tapped shyly at our kitchen door.

"Ahh! I have a brother too, now!" she whispered, her dark eyes on the baby astride my hip. "He is just born. Come see!"

In the dusky interior of a smoky old canvas *tipi* an Indian woman bent over the new baby on her lap. At the noise of our excited entry, the tiny red-brown face puckered up. The mother caught the little nose gently between her thumb and forefinger, and with her palm over the mouth stopped the cry soundlessly. When the baby began to twist for breath she let go a little, but only a little, and at the first sign of another cry she shut the air off again, crooning softly a Cheyenne growing song to make the son straight-limbed and strong of body and heart.

I already knew why none of my small Indian friends made more than a whimper at the greatest hurt. An old grandmother had told me that Indian mothers always shut off the first cry of the newborn, and as often after that as necessary. This is to teach the most important lesson of old Indian life: No one can be permitted to endanger the people; no cry must guide a skulking enemy to the village or spoil a hunt that might mean the winter's meat for a tribe.

But I knew, too, that never in this new baby's life would he be touched by a punishing hand. He would be made equal to the demands of his expanding world without physical chastisement. I remember the stern faces of the Sioux when in the swift heat of temper my father whipped us. These Indians still consider the whites a brutal people who treat their children like enemies that must be bribed or punished or coddled like fragile toys. They believe that children so treated will grow up dependent and immature, and subject to fits of uncontrolled anger within the family circle. They point to the increasing lawlessness and violence of our young people, so often against their elders, a thing unheard of among these Indians.

Our copper-skinned neighbors avoided any overprotection of the young, particularly a mother's favoritism for the eldest son. By custom, the eldest son was provided with a second father, usually a man with a warmhearted wife at whose fireside the boy would spend a great deal of time and whom he could treat with less formality than his mother. Later, if the boy should show some special bent he might select still another man, one fitted to guide those new interests. Once it was a warrior, a hunter, a holy man or an artist. Now it would be a farmer, a cattleman, a mechanic.

When the Indian boy began to crawl no one would cry, "No, no!" and drag him back from the enticing red of the fire. "One must learn from the bite of the flame to let it alone." As he jerked his hand back, whimpering, the boy's eyes would turn in anger not toward any grown up but toward the pretty coals, the source of his pain. He would creep back again, but slower, warily, and soon he would know where warmth became burning.

MARI SANDOZ

By the time the Indian boy across the road was six weeks old he had learned about water, "He must go into the river before he forgets the swimming," the mother told me, an ability she was certain was given to the young of all creatures alike: the cub, the colt, the buffalo calf, the child. The boy swam well before he could walk and so it was safe to let him play around the placid river.

The young Indian's attitude toward girls was established early. "See how the boy is with the women of his lodge and you can know how the young man will be with your daughter," was an old Cheyenne saying. Overfamiliarity has been discouraged since the days in the skin lodges, when perhaps seven or more lived about a winter fire. The father had the place of honor at the back, the youths and boys to his left, the women and girls to the right, with an old woman as keeper of the entrance, seeing all who came and went. Such close living demanded a well-established pattern of conduct if there was to be order and peace during those confining winter months.

The Indian boy sees the religion of his people all about him from the day of his birth. The older men of his family probably still offer the first puff of the council pipe, the first bit of food at each meal, to the sky, the earth and the four winds, which together are the Great Powers in whom man and nature are united in brotherhood. In such a philosophy hatred can never be harbored, not even hatred of an enemy. During the intertribal conflicts of the buffalo days, war prisoners sometimes became wives of chiefs and returned to visit their people with their husbands. Captured men and boys, too, might be taken into the tribe. Sitting Bull's adopted brother was a war captive and honored all his life by the Sioux.

The Indians have added much of this concept and the rituals of the Great Powers to their notion of Christian beliefs. One Sunday morning I went out for wash water from the creek. As I stooped to dip it up I heard Indian singing and the swish of water below me. A young Sioux knelt among the gray-green willows of the bank washing a blue shirt. He lifted it high from the water toward the sky and then dipped it toward the earth and all around, as the pipe and food are offered. Silently I slipped away, and several hours later the young man came riding by, wearing the clean blue shirt. He raised his hand in greeting, palm out, in the old, old gesture of friendship, the left hand because it is nearest the heart and has shed no man's blood. He was on his way to mass at the Mission—in a shirt offered in the old way to the Powers of the world.

Among these peoples there was no evil spirit to be appeased or circumvented. If things did not go well it was not due to supernatural anger but because the people and their leaders were out of tune with the Great Powers. To discover what must be done, men went to fast on high places, hoping for guidance. These Indians still do not take Satan and hell-fire very seriously, or the concept of an avenging God. The idea of building up fear is alien to their philosophy.

The Sioux and Cheyenne had no fear of death and no uneasiness about the dead. Often relatives and friends went to sit at a burial scaffold, now the cemetery, as they would have gone to the fireside of the departed one. Children saw the sickness, the dying, the burial, and often went along to visit the burial place.

Once, on my way home with a bundle of wood, I ran into an old Indian dancing gravely by himself on a little knoll. When he noticed me I started to run, guilty because I had spied on a grownup. But the Indian called me back with the one word, "Granddaughter." With pictures in the dust and sign talk he told me the story of the old woman who lived in the moon that was just rising full out of the east. He showed me the bundle of wood she had hurriedly gathered before the storm that always followed the moon's first waning. Then he talked of why he had come here, where over 50 years ago a great man of his people had been left on a burial scaffold to return to the grass that fed the buffalo who would in turn feed the Indian.

I left the man there, filling his feathered stone pipe, the last of the evening sun on his wrinkled face and his neat, fur-wrapped braids. He was a scarred old warrior come to the burial place of a chief killed by white soldiers. Yet he could call their child "granddaughter" and tell her a story which dignified the detested task of wood-bearing.

MARI SANDOZ

This use of the words "grandson" and "granddaughter" contains, I think, the essence of the Indians' attitude toward the young. The child's first lesson teaches him that in matters of public safety, public good, the individual must subordinate himself to the group. But in return he senses from the start that all his community has an equal responsibility toward him. Every fire will welcome him, every pot will have a little extra for a hungry boy, every ear is open to his griefs, his joys, his aspirations. And as his world expands he finds himself growing with it, into a society that needs no locks against him, no paper to record his word. He is a free man because he has learned to discipline himself, and a happy one because he can discharge his responsibilities to others and to himself as an oriented, intrinsic part of this community, a partner in a wide, encompassing brotherhood.

7

Women in *These Were the Sioux*

Mari Sandoz's Portrayal of Gender

SHANNON D. SMITH

Mari Sandoz's admiration and respect for the Plains Indian way of life is apparent on every page of her 1961 work *These Were the Sioux.* Driven by a need to educate American readers of the history and current plight of Native peoples, her book describes the dignified world of the Sioux.[1] Sandoz's own experiences with the Sioux allowed her to depict, elegantly and honestly, the activities, beliefs, traditions, and coequal roles of women and men that were vital to the survival of Sioux people and culture. Publication of *These Were the Sioux* occurred at an important juncture in western and Native American historical scholarship, as scholars were becoming increasingly aware of their need to expand methodologies and topics to include stories of minorities and women into America's historical narrative. During the previous twenty years, Sandoz had published books and articles employing many of the

9. Unidentified woman, Sandhills, Nebraska. Helen Winter Stauffer Collection 200300100050. Mari Sandoz High Plains Heritage Center.

very methodologies that, in the 1960s, were now being proposed to eliminate cultural bias in historical research. Furthermore, Sandoz dedicated more than a third of *These Were the Sioux* to the prominence and meaning of the roles of Sioux women, well before scholars began to emphasize women of any social or ethnic group in their research. Situating Sandoz in a historiographical context illustrates that her experiences and motives in publishing *These Were the Sioux* place her well ahead of the wave of New Western, "New Indian," and women historians' efforts to incorporate women and minorities into the history of the West.

Sandoz's upbringing in a multicultural environment enabled her to learn about the Sioux with no preconceived sense of superiority. As a young child she found the Sioux to be no more unusual than the colorful palette of "immigrant Poles, Czechs, Irish, Dutch, French, Germans, Danes, Swiss, a few Serbs, a Bulgar, a Mohammedan, a Negro and . . . Texas cowboys" who visited her family's homestead.[2] Most of these neighbors' and guests' words, including those of the Sioux, were foreign to Sandoz, who spoke the Swiss German of her mother. Sandoz literally entered the Sioux world as a child, learning about them "through the slowly forming template of language— oral, mental, and bodily" as proscribed by future ethnohistorians.[3] Sandoz was precociously inquisitive and learned a great deal from her Sioux friends. She became adept at communicating with sign language and got to know many of the Indians who frequently camped near the Sandoz family home on the Niobrara River. As an adult she drew upon these childhood experiences to develop a keen awareness of the Plains Indian worldview.

When Sandoz wrote *These Were the Sioux*, she had more than three decades of experience researching and writing about Plains Indians. Her earliest writing had focused on the struggles of white settlers, such as her father. During the 1920s, as she studied history and literature at the University of Nebraska, Sandoz wrote several versions of what would ultimately become her first major work, *Old Jules*, and several articles that told stories of early homesteaders and ranchers.[4]

SHANNON D. SMITH

In 1930 she spent three weeks with her friend Eleanor Hinman, exploring the Indian reservations of North and South Dakota, Wyoming, and Montana. The two covered more than three thousand miles in a Model T Ford Coupe as they camped on the reservations and interviewed elderly survivors of the United States–Sioux wars. Sandoz's biographer, Helen Winter Stauffer, describes this trip as an epiphany that "opened a hitherto unexplored aspect of history and literature to her." Sandoz suddenly realized that her unique position—having grown up with Indians and homesteaders—enabled her to, in Stauffer's words, "view their culture from the inside, as a native of the region, as well as from the outside, as a scholar, and thus could present a valuable insight into their past."[5]

She began to add stories of the Indians to her growing collection of rejected articles. She also continued her research, working on a book about the Oglala Sioux chief Red Cloud for the Nebraska State Historical Society in 1931 and returning to the reservations with Hinman again in 1931 and 1932. After publishing *Old Jules* to critical acclaim in 1935, Sandoz wrote articles and novels with white protagonists, but spent most of the decade trying to understand the Indian perspective and fine-tune her ability to present it. The results of her work, including *Crazy Horse* (1942) and *Cheyenne Autumn* (1953), along with dozens of articles and short stories, established Sandoz as an expert in the history and culture of the Plains Indians.

During the 1930s, '40s, and '50s, while other scholars continued to use Euro-American records to write "white man's history" about Native Americans, Sandoz employed sources and techniques that anthropologists, historians, and ethnohistorians would "discover" years later. Sandoz clearly understood the importance of oral tradition. She conducted interviews and used oral narratives as sources, but she also developed an unorthodox writing style to simulate Sioux oral tradition, using simple, carefully selected words assembled in a particular rhythmic pattern to convey Native American concepts and words for which no English counterparts existed. She hoped her technique would "suggest something of [the Indian's] innate nature, something of his relationship to the earth and the sky and all that is between."[6]

Sandoz understood the profound connection the Sioux held with the land and worked hard to convey their sense of the land to her readers. Part of her research involved walking and camping on the lands where Sioux history took place in order to portray it faithfully in her writings. Sandoz also consulted maps, art, and artifacts to support and analyze her extensive research of traditional sources at archives across the country. Helen Stauffer recalls the words of a critic who, in 1961, noted the "dual authority of participation and research" apparent in Sandoz's work.[7] This unique combination of personal experience and professional expertise situated Sandoz years ahead of her academic counterparts in Indian history.

As a field of study, the history of the American West fell out of favor among scholars in the late 1950s. Many disputed the underlying exceptionalist thesis, introduced by Frederick Jackson Turner, in 1893, that celebrated a westward progression of American civilization across the North American continent dominated by white, Anglo-Saxon men. A newer generation of scholars considered Turner's exceptionalist theory racist, sexist, and imperialist in its depiction of the American West, and western history was viewed as lacking relevance to the pressing social issues of the day, such as civil rights, the cold war, and feminism. In their analysis of mid-century western history, William Cronon, George Miles, and Jay Gitlin observed that "as historians of the 1950s and 1960s sought to explore the problems that mattered most to them, the western past seemed at best an irrelevant distraction."[8] Scholars who still found relevance in western history increasingly challenged Turner's "frontier thesis" and shifted scholarly focus to more progressive topics, calling for studies of women and minorities to fill gaping holes in the narrative of America's history. By the late 1980s Patricia Nelson Limerick, Richard White, William Cronon, and Donald Woster helped usher in a "new" western history, leading the call for western historians to unmask the old frontier thesis and incorporate the voices of marginalized groups—including women and Native Americans—into the story.[9]

When western history headed toward its nadir in the 1950s, scholarship on Native Americans hit a low point as well. David Edmunds writes that "Native Americans remained marginalized in American history and many academic historians considered Native American history to be 'popular history' or 'cowboys and Indians,' not worthy of serious research."[10] The few historians who did write about Native Americans based their studies on primary sources written by white recorders, generally the very people who sought and often secured control over, or destruction of, Native peoples.[11] The cultural biases of these writers, too, frequently intensified when they analyzed and presented Native culture from their privileged position as white male historians. Consequently, Native Americans figured into the historical narrative as minor players reacting or responding to Euro-American initiatives. "They remained," in Edmunds's words, "the supporting cast in a drama whose plot and leading roles were European."[12]

A major shift in Native American scholarship occurred in the mid-1940s with the creation of the Indian Claims Commission. Until then, most Native American research had been the province of anthropology departments, a place where "old men in plaid shirts and dirty boots attended to all the 'primitive others of the world,' who constituted, at best, exotic footnotes to the real history of 'civilized' movers and shakers."[13] The Indian Claims Commission, created by an act of Congress, in August 1946, to adjudicate land claims by Native American tribes, brought anthropologists and historians together to provide expert testimony for cases that came before the commission. Resolution of these land claim cases required preparation of in-depth reports concerning American Indian land use and tenure. Claims to title of the lands in question required evaluation based on the testimony of tribal members and on research conducted by anthropologists, archeologists, and historians. The complex litigation, involving more than eight hundred cases representing hundreds of millions of dollars, employed the services of anthropologists and historians to determine whether specific tribes occupied the lands in question. Because evidence of the *contemporary* practices and locations of the tribes was inadmissible, anthropologists turned to sources used by historians—the documentary record of Euro-Americans. "Yet the questions the anthropologists asked of the historical sources," writes James Axtell, "were not the kinds of questions that historians would ask, but were drawn from typically ethnological concerns, acquired from the anthropologists' own training and field work."[14] This process, viewing historical sources from within the cultural context of the subject, became known as ethnohistory.

In 1952 historically minded anthropologists organized the American Indian Ethnohistoric Conference, later named the American Society for Ethnohistory. Conceived as a method to "portray native peoples in their own right, acting for their own reasons in light of their own cultural norms and values," ethnohistory combined the fieldwork techniques of anthropology with the documentary research techniques of historians.[15] Searching beyond Euro-American documentary texts, ethnohistorians collected and studied oral history, artifacts, maps, languages, and other nontraditional sources to develop a new, Indian-centered narrative.[16] During the next twenty years, ethnohistorians dramatically increased the quantity and quality of scholarship on Native American history. Acknowledging that Indian history did not begin at the moment of white contact, they began to reconstruct precontact historical narratives. Instead of depicting Indians as hapless victims of colonial policies, scholars researched and documented successful strategies Native Americans used to manipulate and adapt to colonial controls. Ethnohistory developed narratives of cultural change, placing Native peoples at the center of a new western narrative showing them as active agents, rather than unwitting pawns, in their struggle with Euro-American imperialism.

Building on the work of Franz Boaz in the 1920s, ethnohistorians sought to understand beliefs and activities through an individual's

SHANNON D. SMITH

own culture, replacing long-held ethnocentric analyses that judged other cultures solely by the researcher's own cultural values and standards.[17] James Axtell describes the profound importance of the new scholarly approach, writing, "Like all students of 'otherness,' ethnohistorians must also try to understand each culture . . . on its own terms, according to its own cultural code, because that is the only way to understand why people in the past acted as they did."[18] To get into the minds of their historical subjects, they must take nothing for granted. "Ideally, every ethnohistorian would enter his or her historical country like a child newly born to the natives," Axtell continues, "through the slowly forming template of language—oral, mental, and, bodily."[19] Without having ever participated in this ethnohistorical debate, Mari Sandoz had, for decades, been using these now "cutting edge" methods, employing nontraditional Native American sources and cultural relevance in her research and writing on Native Americans.

Sandoz's inclusion of Native women in her study of the Sioux Indians is a harbinger of scholarly trends, preceding the feminist-inspired study of women's history. Betty Friedan's pathbreaking work *The Feminist Mystique* (1963) helped launch a new field of inquiry called women's studies. Scholarship on women in the West slowly emerged, initially focused on the lives and experiences of white, middle-class settlers. Early publications were a mixed blessing.[20] Despite the welcome addition of women into the western narrative, accurate depictions were replaced with a "lofty rhetoric distorting western women beyond recognition," such as the saintly "Madonnas of the Plains" and the civilizing "Gentle Tamers."[21] The few women who made it into the robust, virile depiction of westward expansion, like Calamity Jane and Annie Oakley, did so on a masculine stage. During the 1980s, as historians of western women expanded their inquiry to include African American, Asian, and Hispanic women, research on American Indian women continued to lag. Glenda Riley suggests one reason is that scholars, believing source materials were sparse, remained pessimistic about uncovering new information to support their work.[22] Another reason involved the misconception that Plains Indians were not important. Patricia Albers described the predilection in American society to associate Indianness with masculinity. "It is the male-dominated universe of native diplomacy, warfare, and hunting," Albers observes, "that has captured the attention of national image-makers."[23]

In this erroneous portrayal, Indian women had little value within the tribe, their roles served only as the "extras" or background labor for the more significant activities of the men. This has been true of fictional portrayals in film and print as well as nonfiction from the early recorders up through twentieth-century writings of historians and anthropologists. Influenced by a male perspective on women's passive and inferior position, Native American women's activities have historically been either trivialized or ignored. Albers locates the problem with critiquing Native gender roles through a non-Native lens, writing, "Many ethnographic descriptions, for example, portray the work of Plains Indian women as menial and monotonous—a view clearly originating from Euro-American ideas on the value of household labor."[24] It was not until the 1980s that historians of Native American women began to create a significant base of scholarship, "smashing the stock images and stereotypes that had so long shrouded them."[25]

Sandoz had begun debunking misguided images of Native women more than twenty years earlier. In *These Were the Sioux,* Sandoz explained that Indian women's tasks had purpose and value. She informed readers that, as the tribe moved between camps, women performed vital functions by carrying bundles and supervising transportation of household goods, as this freed men to hunt and protect the tribe. Sandoz disputed the idea that women's work was menial labor required to support innately lazy Native American men. "The arrogant and superior white traveler, the superficial observer," Sandoz writes, "assumed from this that the Sioux woman was a drudge, the Indian man a lazy dog—but not too lazy to make a living for his people with crude bow and lance for thousands of years."[26] Her association with Native peoples since childhood allowed her to see beyond ethnocentric stereotypes.

Sandoz described the matrilineal tradition of a Plains Indian man joining the wife's family and assuming a position of importance through her family's prestige. For this he was to contribute to the family's assets with his good reputation and a respectable amount of horses. "To the European who welcomed a dowry with his bride," Sandoz informs her readers, "this custom of the man bringing the dowry seemed very odd and somehow degrading, but, curiously, degrading to the woman."[27] She also rebutted the typical presentation of Plains Indian women as promiscuous, pointing out the "firm belief that when women lost their virtue the buffalo would disappear, the people starve. To the Sioux not only the honor but the very existence of the tribe lay in the moccasin tracks of their women."[28]

Sandoz tackled controversial subjects avoided until the 1980s as she described the simple yet effective strategies used by the Sioux to handle divorce, infidelity, and spousal abuse.[29] She pointed out the equally severe punishments for attempted rape and for wrongfully challenging a woman's virginity.[30] She dedicated five pages of *These Were the Sioux* to the cultural importance and prestige of the puberty ceremony after a young woman's "first menstrual time."[31] Sandoz introduces readers to Native accommodating views of gendered behavior. Rather than strict guidelines for women and men's behaviors, a Eurocentric construction, Native cultures accepted men and women according to their individual natures. Euro-Americans could not fathom why berdaches, whom they described as a "woman-man" who "failed to make his way to genuine manhood," held an honored position in Sioux society. Nor could they understand why a tribe would easily accept a strong-hearted woman.[32] Sandoz's unique perspective on women and gender, shaped by her own life experiences, enabled her to treat these topics with dignity and respect two decades before academic historians approached these important issues.

Having succeeded in the male-dominated world of publishing and surrounding herself with other successful women, Sandoz clearly felt that women were as capable as men. According to Stauffer, "To her [Sandoz], the division between the sexes in American society was artificial. . . . She stressed more than once that gender differences in people were less significant than other characteristics."[33] All of these factors served to sharpen her awareness of gender and make her recognize the importance of women in other cultures. The way of life of the Sioux, when seen through the lens of Sandoz's own beliefs about gender identity, had to include both men and women.

While Sandoz's own cultural and gender sensitivity provided the basis for *These Were the Sioux,* her motivation for publication came from external influences. Her disgust with the United States' destructive policy of termination and relocation in the 1950s inspired Sandoz to write this tribute to the Sioux way of life, increasingly under threat of disappearing forever. The work of the Indian Claims Commission was the foundation of the termination policy. Prior to 1946, a tribe could bring suit against the federal government only with the special permission of Congress, but the United States' involvement in the Nuremberg Trials at the end of World War II led to a change in policy. These trials were going to be prosecuted on the theory that the accused Nazis were men who "implemented policies which led to death, disease and starvation."[34] The definitions of genocide, war crimes, and persecution as negotiated and defined by the Allies in preparation for the trials sounded disconcertingly similar to United States Indian Policy for the past two centuries.[35] To divert attention from this obvious comparison, Congress passed the Indian Claims Commission Act in 1946 to hear all tribal "grievances" concerning land claims. The act stipulated that "stolen lands could not be returned, they could only he paid for," meaning any attempt to seek justice through the commission meant specifically losing title to the land in question.[36] Rather than redressing past inequities, the act enabled the United States to legally acquire what had been illegally expropriated from Native

SHANNON D. SMITH

people in direct violation of signed treaties, casting a facade of legitimacy over past wrongdoing.

The Indian Claims Commission Act paved the way for the institution of the termination and relocation policy of the Eisenhower administration in the 1950s. House Resolution 1063, more commonly known as the Federal Relocation Policy, used Congressional action to unilaterally dissolve 109 Indigenous nations between 1953 and 1958.[37] The reasons for the implementation of this plan were twofold. First, a longstanding resentment to John Collier's Indian New Deal, put in place under President Franklin D. Roosevelt, encouraged Federal legislators, after Collier's removal as head of the Bureau of Indian Affairs, to construct a law designed to "get the government out of the Indian business," by stipulating that the Indians would be scattered through "relocation programs" to the cities and thereby transferring independence onto a people trained to total dependency.[38] The second reason followed a longstanding federal agenda of expropriating Indian land for the government's and non-Indian people's use. Relocated Indians found themselves dumped into cities that had little or no use for them; those who stayed on the reservation lost the meager government support they had depended on for survival. Native Americans found themselves in an untenable situation, living in increasing poverty on the reservation and, for those whose reservations had been dissolved, resigned to urban life, often in ghettos.

While the nation at large may have overlooked the distress of Native people, Sandoz was acutely aware of their plight. In February of 1952 she published an article, "What I Learned from the Indians," in the *Denver Post*'s *Empire Magazine*.[39] In May it was condensed and published in *Reader's Digest* as "What the Sioux Taught Me."[40] She hoped these articles would educate the American public to the fine characteristics of Native people, as well as draw attention to their current problems. The public reception of these articles convinced Sandoz she had a platform, encouraging her to choose *Cheyenne Autumn* over *Miss Morissa* as her next book to bring to market. She also wrote to politicians, appeared on TV shows, and spoke at meetings of the Association for American Indian Affairs.[41] Over the next ten years, she corresponded with friends, fans, and anyone who she felt would push for Indian land reform.

Her concern and lobbying on behalf of Plains Indians grew as their conditions worsened. On February 12, 1960, Sandoz wrote directly to the secretary of the interior, fellow Nebraskan Fred A. Seaton, appealing for assistance for the Northern Cheyenne Reservation in Lame Deer, Montana. She believed that the real obstacle to their self-sufficiency and escape from poverty was "the people on and off the Reservation who wanted the range, the oil, the coal" of tribal lands. She claimed that the Bureau of Indian Affairs office in Lame Deer was another obstacle and that when she had gone there to seek assistance for her Indian friends she "was met with less than common courtesy by a couple of the key men."[42] She and her longtime friend Charles Barrett of Long Island, Maine, wrote many letters to politicians to draw attention to Indian issues. In April 1960, Barrett wrote to Sandoz five times informing her of his letters to "Senator Kennedy" and "Vice President Nixon" and several other politicians. He sent her a copy of a letter he received from the Bureau of Indian Affairs assuring him that conditions were not as bad as he was being led to believe. On April 13 Sandoz wrote back to Barrett: "Don't let the Indian affairs form letter throw you."[43] Two weeks later Barrett received the same form letter from Senator Kennedy's office.

On May 24, 1960, Helen Hector, associate editor for *Reader's Digest*, gave Sandoz another opportunity to draw the public's attention to the past injustice and current situation of the Plains Indians. Hector wrote to Sandoz, "I was rereading one of my favorite stories in the Digest, your article, 'What the Sioux Taught Me,' and it set me to wondering if you are doing anything else along this line. There is so much we can learn from the Indians, from the pioneers. From your close association with the Indians, is there another 'What the Sioux Taught Me' piece from the angle of religion, art of living, death?"[44] Sandoz leapt at the opportunity, telling Hector she had already accumulated material to make another article "from the angle of religion, art of living and death," and that she was "letting it ripen and deepen a bit in content and meaning."[45] Arrangements were made through Sandoz's agent and she quickly submitted a manuscript.

On September 26, Hector sent a lengthy critique to Sandoz's agent stating that *Reader's Digest* was disappointed in the article. They felt it was a "rather sprawling essay approach" and wondered if it was "a feeler to see what we did want." Hector said that the only possible salvage would be for Sandoz to "tackle it from another point of view." She proceeded to identify several other angles and approaches that would tie the article into modern times, similar to the 1952 article's focus on raising children. Hector also stated that in some spots "things sound a bit mystic and I think would leave the reader merely baffled instead of making a point with him."[46] In the end, she wondered if Sandoz had the material or inclination to rework the article to their specifications.

Sandoz was livid when she read Hector's letter, and responded immediately, making it clear to Hector she had no intention of reworking the piece. Opening with an apology for her article taking up so much of their time, she said that their criticism was "just." She then stated, "Unfortunately, any article about the Sioux 'from the angle of religion, art of living, death' as your letter of May 24 suggested might well have the flaws you found." Sandoz explained that the main difficulty with their suggestions was the "vast difference in the Sioux situation" since the 1952 article. "Almost any example or anecdote to illustrate the good of Sioux life has become unsuited to a periodical of wide circulation because it would suggest a real or implied criticism of the present administration which, the Indians say, 'has taken away everything we had left and given us only alcohol to drown our misery.'" She described the 1953 legislation, House Resolution 1063—the Federal Relocation Policy—and its devastating consequences. "Practically any example of the good life I might have given you could have been challenged by the realities of the new degradation." She acknowledged that the Northern Cheyenne's situation had improved marginally, due in part to the publication of her *Cheyenne Autumn*, but stated, "The Sioux situation is still so tragic I could weep if those Indians hadn't taught me not to cry." She enclosed copies of editorials against HR 1063 and acerbically concluded, "I am sorry I couldn't get a little sympathy for [the Sioux] through the article."[47] If Sandoz was livid with their clearly uninformed criticism, *Reader's Digest*'s response six weeks later must have made her apoplectic.

On November 17, Hector wrote that Sandoz's letter had moved her; she had held on to it to show to her managing editor, who had been away. She wondered if they couldn't do something about the Sioux's situation but, "The consensus here was: that the Association of American Indian Affairs according to a recent publication, seems more optimistic about the trend; and that Seaton has tried to remedy the situation and Kennedy has promised to. So, I guess we wait awhile."[48] The same form letter that Sandoz and Barrett had received from the political machine in Washington had been sent to placate the editors at *Reader's Digest* and had essentially stopped publication of her article.

Sandoz had already determined that the changes *Reader's Digest* wanted "were not, upon a long mulling over, the kind that I can make in material about the American Indian. . . . It's full of good material that has been lost to the Indians since the old buffalo hunters have died off, and so I am duty bound to see that it reaches print, in the form that it should have."[49] Instead, in December Sandoz negotiated a contract to publish *These Were the Sioux* as a book with Hastings House, one of her favorite publishers. By March she had completed the first draft and by April she had completed revisions and supplied artwork from Amos Bad Heart Bull and Kills Two.

Published in the fall of 1961, Sandoz was pleased with the appearance of *These Were the Sioux* and sure it would be a good book for the Christmas market—and the critics agreed. More importantly, she

SHANNON D. SMITH

hoped the book would help readers see the beauty and humanity of a culture under attack by the government's pernicious policy of termination and relocation. Her knowledge of the Sioux, based on a sensitivity to culture and gender far ahead of scholarly trends, ensured she would deliver a sensitive portrayal of their practices and beliefs, and guaranteed Sioux women would be included in the story. After the *Reader's Digest* fiasco, when she proposed the book to editor Walter Frese at Hastings House, she said, "I envision this as a small book . . . not a story for young people but for people, young and old. Really a sort of special book, if I can write it well enough."[50] She did, and it is.

NOTES

1. "Sioux" refers to a confederacy of several tribes that speak three different dialects, the Lakota, Dakota, and Nakota. The Lakota, also known as the Teton Sioux, are comprised of seven tribal bands, including the Oglala Lakota of the Pine Ridge Reservation, and were the peoples with whom Sandoz had the most personal experience. Sandoz knew the difference between bands and tribes of the northern plains, but she used the name "Sioux" as it was most commonly known by the general public.

2. Sandoz, *These Were the Sioux* (1961; repr., Lincoln: University of Nebraska Press, 1985), 9.

3. Axtell, "Ethnohistory of Native America," 14.

4. Sandoz, *Old Jules.*

5. Stauffer, *Story Catcher of the Plains,* 79.

6. Sandoz, *Crazy Horse,* xxvi.

7 Stauffer, *Story Catcher of the Plains,* 238.

8. Cronon, Miles, and Gitlin, "Becoming West," 4.

9. Limerick, *Legacy of Conquest.*

10. Edmunds, "Native Americans, New Voices,"721.

11. Axtell, "Ethnohistory of Native America," 14.

12. Edmunds, "Native Americans, New Voices,"720.

13. Axtell, "Ethnohistory of Native America," 11.

14. Axtell, "Ethnohistory of Early America," 110–14.

15. Berkhofer, "Cultural Pluralism versus Ethnocentrism," 36.

16. Axtell, "An Historian's Viewpoint," 3–4.

17. Boas, *Franz Boas Reader*.

18. Axtell, "Ethnohistory of Native America," 13.

19. Axtell, "Ethnohistory of Native America," 14.

20. Brown, *Gentle Tamers*; Larson, "Dolls, Vassals, and Drudges"; Stoeltje, "'Help-mate for Man Indeed.'"

21. Jensen and Miller, "The Gentle Tamers Revisited."

22. Riley, "Historiography of American Indian and Other Western Women," 44; Albers, "New Perspectives on Plains Indian Women," 6.

23. Albers, "New Perspectives on Plains Indian Women," 2.

24. Albers, "New Perspectives on Plains Indian Women," 4.

25. Riley, "Historiography of American Indian and Other Western Women,"47.

26. Sandoz, *These Were the Sioux*, 102–3.

27. Sandoz, *These Were the Sioux*, 79.

28. Sandoz, *These Were the Sioux*, 72–73.

29. Sandoz, *These Were the Sioux*, 49, 81–83; See also Weist, "Plains Indian Women," and Albers and Medicine, eds. *Hidden Half*. Ella Deloria brings up the topics of divorce, infidelity, and spousal abuse in *Waterlilly*. Manuscript complete in 1942, but not published until 1988.

30. Sandoz, *These Were the Sioux*, 56, 93.

31. Sandoz, *These Were the Sioux*, 94–98.

32. Sandoz, *These Were the Sioux*, 70–72. For a more nuanced view on berdaches and also for strong-hearted women, see Ford, "Native American Women."

33. Sandoz, *Letters*, xxxii.

34. William Manchester, quoted in Cook-Lynn, *Anti-Indianism in Modern America*, 29.

35. Cook-Lynn, *Anti-Indianism in Modern America*, 29.

36. Cook-Lynn, *Anti-Indianism in Modern America*, 29.

37. Fixico, *Termination and Relocation*, 98–111.

38. Matthiessen, *In the Spirit of Crazy Horse*, 28.

39. Sandoz, "What I Learned from the Indians," 8–9.

40. Sandoz, "What the Sioux Taught Me," 121–24.

41. Stauffer, *Story Catcher of the Plains*, 186.

42. Mari Sandoz to Fred A. Seaton, February 12, 1960, MS00032, Mari Sandoz Collection, Archives and Special Collections, University of Nebraska–Lincoln Libraries. (Hereafter cited as Sandoz Collection).

43. Mari Sandoz to Charles Barrett, April 13, 1960, MS00032, Sandoz Collection.

44. Helen Firstbrook Hector to Mari Sandoz, May 24, 1960, MS00032, Sandoz Collection.

45. Mari Sandoz to Helen Hector, May 29, 1960, MS00032, Sandoz Collection.

46. Helen Firstbrook Hector to Elizabeth R. Otis, September 26, 1960, MS00032, Sandoz Collection.

47. Mari Sandoz to Helen Hector, October 5, 1960, MS00032, Sandoz Collection.

48. Helen Firstbrook Hector to Mari Sandoz, November 17, 1960, MS00032, Sandoz Collection.

49. Mari Sandoz to Jim Carr, September 29, 1960, MS00032, Sandoz Collection.

50. Mari Sandoz to Walter Frese [c. 1960], MS00032, Sandoz Collection.

10. Mari Sandoz. Helen Winter Stauffer Collection 2003001004. Mari Sandoz High Plains Heritage Center.

In 2014 the Mari Sandoz Heritage Society initiated a competitive scholarship, the Sandoz Research Award, to encourage research emphasizing new insights on Mari Sandoz or ways to explore her life or her work. The award, open to undergraduate and graduate students, encourages explorations into topics that can include, but are not limited to, feminism, American Indian issues, activism, environmental issues, and social/cultural issues. Jillian Wenburg was selected as the first recipient of the Sandoz Research Award. The following essay is based on her research lecture that she presented to at the Mari Sandoz Symposium at Chadron State College in 2015.

8

Sandoz Constructing Women with "Well-Knit Bone and Nerve"

Androgyny and Activism on the Great Plains

JILLIAN L. WENBURG

"I'm not used to seeing pioneers in the flesh and Hollywood's version had not prepared me for this one. Mari Sandoz is not strapping, she is wiry; her strength is not that of muscle but of well-knit bone and nerve. She is painfully thin, with her high staccato Midwestern voice," Edward Weeks, from *Atlantic Monthly Press*, said of Mari Sandoz.[1] Her attitude is reflected in her appearance. She cared little for frivolities, ate for sufficiency rather than indulging, and dressed for utilitarian purposes. Her discussion of pioneers and the Nebraska plains is similar to her appearance: nervy, unembellished, and just as efficient. Her high staccato voice is a mirror reflection of how her literary works resonated, with sharpness, crisp assertion, and command. She instructed readers and directed them in ways to act. Specifically, her hands demonstrate an abundance of the androgynous traits she valued: "They were the hands of a farmer— broad, calloused, knobby. When you looked at her hands, you *knew* Mari Sandoz had worked mighty hard in the fields and the barns." Her hands are significant, showing she valued difficult, consistent hard work and physically demanding labor, demonstrative of both conviction and perseverance.

If Sandoz's attitude can present as cocky and off-putting, her hands are problematic for that reading. They show Sandoz was not just another midwestern farm woman out to publish a few books and papers to fire up her community and make a name for herself. She was not a polished Omaha debutante representing at the Ak-Sar-Ben ball.[2] Nor was she a figurehead rodeo rider from the western counties. Her hands told her story of a hardworking woman, striving to subsist as a single woman in the 1930s. Seeing Sandoz as only an impudent voice does her work and the woman a disservice. It misses what drove her as well as what she was able to drive to, which is what is most significant about her work. She established a redefinition of gendered behavior in her literary works, which called to action a constructed, ambiguous, gendered identity.[3]

Her gender ideal was that there need not be an ideal, neither masculine nor feminine.[4] Her writing reformulated the notion of gender and reduced its importance so that the most capable individual achieved success because of his or her abilities, not because of an innate characteristic. Sandoz showed women succeeding outside of the traditional midwestern gender norms of the 1930s in order to develop a dialogue about gender roles, allowing room for women to become ruthless power-hungry dictators, autonomous frontier doctors, or assertive authors.

In the same way that Judith Butler negotiates how "it becomes impossible to separate out 'gender' from the political and cultural intersections in which it is invariably produced and maintained," Sandoz shows how an ambiguous gender identity can be beneficial.[5] Thus, just as Butler confirms that gender cannot be explicit, Sandoz shows how gender can be manipulated and, even more interesting, performed. Sandoz's gender agenda lies in demonstrating how her vision of womanhood can permit women to achieve more personally and as a part of the larger community they operate under.

Sandoz understood the perils of power; in her girlhood, she had seen firsthand the suffering of plains' women. In her writing, she conceptualized revised gender constructions based upon androgynous characteristics and even created an, at times, androgynous identity for herself. Contesting this gendered identity allowed Sandoz to show

JILLIAN L. WENBURG

that women could achieve more; she did not rely on the fallacy of tradition that women were substandard thinkers or contributors. She strove for equality. Some critics chastised Sandoz for her work, with one *Capital City* critic noting, "One should pay her the compliment of saying that she thinks and expresses herself with the untrammeled vigor of a man, but would have to add that she thinks and expresses herself like an angry and not particularly well-balanced man."[6] She continued writing with that "vigor," showing attributes of masculinity and femininity that required an equalization in order to keep society in balance and from tipping into corruption and injustice. Perhaps more importantly, she showed identity need not be identified by gender stereotypes; identity appeared separate from gender.

Four texts evidence how Sandoz conceived of a gender ideal and what values she advanced. The identities in these texts run the gendered gamut from motherhood to masculine and feminine to feminist.[7] Her female protagonists provide models for emulation, such as in the case of Abigail (*Capital City*) and Marie (*Old Jules*). A model representing the difficulty of balance emerges in the tale of Morissa (*Miss Morissa*). Mary (*Old Jules*) and Gulla (*Slogum House)* represent models to avoid. *Old Jules, Capital City, Miss Morissa: Doctor of the Gold Trail,* and *Slogum House* demonstrate the diverse ways in which Sandoz conceived of gender, the values she found admirable or used as cautionary tales. And yet Sandoz's novels maintain discursive spaces that allow readers to develop their own conceptions toward gender issues. Sandoz readers find frontier women are not always disciplined helpmeets, but are active change agents for their families and society, a concept not delineated in any western history monograph effectively until Sandra Myres's 1982 *Westering Women and the Frontier Experience 1800–1915.*[8] She broke through to the masses with her work, ultimately spreading historical knowledge in a more palatable way, even if the reading audience didn't anticipate that knowledge.

Sandoz critically portrays the nineteenth-century ideal of femininity and womanhood for her readers' consideration and identifies troubles that befall this flawed societal model. Although this could be interpreted as a feminist agenda, in Sandoz's case, it is more so a humanist agenda: advancing equal rights for all, regardless of gender.[9] Sandoz remained detached from the women's rights movement. In fact, when friend Estelle Laughlin wrote to her about her support of the Equal Rights Amendment, Sandoz decried the response of government officials: "The way to further the cause of women was not by breaking down favorable legislation but to get equally favorable legislation passed for men. . . . Truly restrictive legislation against any group, sex, color or religion irks me and on that sort of thing Mrs. Babcock could count on me to face even the menial fuzz-buddies in the senate."[10]

Sandoz clearly advocates for rulings that promote men and women equally. She argued that some specific legislation served to separate them, promoting special treatment for one party over another and not furthering the goal of equality for all. In Sandoz's works, as in this letter, she favors a simpler government that does not isolate one gender or another, but works to cement the notion of equality on a communitarian level. If legislation needed to be written for women, Sandoz argued, write in "equally favorable legislation" for men.[11]

The act of exclusion and isolation created problems, Sandoz insisted. She was a proud promoter of women, but did not want a particular gender treated specially or called out individually; she wanted only equal treatment. In a libertarian move, Sandoz argued that differentiating between the sexes only served to divide society further rather than unite it. This binary created dual and often battling agendas with cross purposes. Sandoz saw how class separation was dividing the country and thought separation by gender would only create further divides in the United States. She saw the debate between male and female equality limiting intellectuals and the nation from advancement.[12] Sandoz was ahead of her time in her consideration of gender politics, anticipating ideas popular with third-wave feminism and postmodernism.

Female characters in Sandoz's works demonstrate that she valued androgynous attributes such as a strong identity, integrity, convictions, intellectualism, independence, perseverance, and agency. Her characters run a spectrum from ultrafeminine to hypermasculine. Sandoz does not advocate for either end of the spectrum, but instead demonstrates how a cohesive balance of these characteristics is the ideal.

The character of Mary, in *Old Jules*, the biography of Sandoz's father, demonstrates her view of ultrafeminism. *Old Jules* is based upon her life story, and in it, Mary, Sandoz's mother, filled the role of the farmer and helpmeet on the Sandoz ranch.[13] She maintained a consistent worry about the farm and food on the table, a very feminine characteristic.[14] Her work was never done; she had a number of responsibilities for the household in addition to her numerous frequent pregnancies: "Her hands blistered, calloused, and then grew horny; her back ached, but if she worked hard enough and long enough, she could sleep."[15] Jules seldom acknowledged or thanked Mary for her work and seemed concerned only with his own accomplishments.[16] Mary embodied stereotypical female submissive characteristics.

Mary entered the story arriving alone. She had traveled to the United States from Switzerland, to homestead the Nebraska plains with her brother, Jacob, but he failed to meet her as arranged at the Rushville train station.[17] She proceeded on by herself, meeting Old Jules, the land locator who had agreed to help the brother and sister stake their claim, at the train station. While independent to some degree, she still relied upon the locator, Jules, to see her to the end of her journey. Jules took Mary to his house; and after spending several days there, she agreed to marry this stranger. He was very protective and would not allow her to integrate with her neighbors. After attending a dance together, Old Jules became filled with jealous rage watching Mary dance with others. He left without her, and he met her at home with "a rifle across his knee." She acquiesced to the demand for submissiveness, a part of ultrafemininity, and "never went to another dance."[18] Clearly, Jules not only expected but required Mary to embody feminine behavior.

Old Jules was difficult to live with in many other respects. He rarely, if ever, praised Mary for her efforts, required extra tending due to his leg handicap, was presumptuous, perfectionist, and demanded his way. At breakfast, he wanted three eggs, regardless of how they were acquired. As Mari noted, her mother "fed her hens hot mash, hoping for an egg or two a day for Jules's breakfast. He always ate three, complaining at the rye coffee instead of chocolate. He never noticed what the rest had."[19] Sandoz used Old Jules as a warning about the kind of mistreatment that women, not just Mary, were enduring.

Old Jules did not confine his violence only to his wife. Perhaps one of the harshest examples of Jules's treatment was his physical abuse of the children. Sandoz writes, "When little Marie was three months old and ill with summer complaint, her cries awakened Jules. . . . He whipped the child until she lay blue and trembling as a terrorized small animal. When Mary dared she snatched the baby from him and carried her into the night and did not return until the bright day."[20] Mary, inevitably afraid of Jules, took her child away from him to safety, despite risking his further wrath when she returned. Yet she did return to Jules despite this violence, indicating that her reliance upon men and ultrafemininity did not protect her from violence or enable her to escape this social injustice.

The only option for escape that Mary considers at one point is suicide. When she asked Jules to help her castrate a large calf, Old Jules got kicked in the process. Sandoz describes what happened next, as Old Jules threatened to kill Mary, and how "Mary ran through the door, past the children and straight to the poison drawer. It stuck, came free, the bottles flying over the floor. Her face furrowed in despair, blood dripping from her face and her hand where she had been struck with the wire whip, the woman snatched up a bottle, struggled with the cork, pulling at it with her teeth. The grandmother was upon her, begging, pleading, clutching at the red bottle with the crossbones."[21] We can see here how this

JILLIAN L. WENBURG

ultrafeminine woman did not see a way out, a way to fight against the man who held power physically and legally against her; at that moment, taking her own life seemed her only escape.

While Sandoz presents Mary as an example of how an extreme adherence to femininity is problematic, Marie, her daughter and Sandoz's autobiographical doppelganger, demonstrates a balanced androgyny. In contrast to her mother, Marie maintained a balance of characteristics, which allowed her to navigate her difficult family life and ultimately achieve success. Marie was taught to hunt, skin, and identify plants, and "Jules taught them useful things."[22] Marie was not just trained as a useful tomboy outside; she was designated as the official mother in training, responsible for cooking and care-taking. She quickly understood that this advanced role was required for survival in her family home.[23]

In addition to learning both male and female skills, there are numerous references to Marie's ability to transcend her environment through intellectualism. Marie strived to achieve skills that would allow her to leave the West and become more productive. When other kids would play at recess, Marie stayed and studied: "You should run out and play. You're so peaked-looking," the serious young schoolma'am tried to tell her kindly. "I got to study," Marie defended herself fiercely.[24] Even when Marie was sick with yellow jaundice and forced to stay home, Sandoz recollected her determination to attend school, writing, "I got to go—they'll all get ahead of me."[25] Marie struggled to catch up and keep up with her peers, especially since, when she had gotten to school, she spoke little English, only Swiss German, and a bit of Polish. Yet, she excelled in reading and earned a reputation all around the Sandhills for her unquenchable thirst for learning.[26] Marie took her studies seriously and despite spotty attendance, illness, snow blindness, caring for the children, and numerous other deterrents, managed to pass her eighth-grade examination.

Marie then slipped away to Rushville to take the teacher's exam-ination, something Old Jules would not have permitted had he known her plans. He was not pleased about her passing the teacher's exam; Sandoz writes, "When Jules heard what she had done he was violent: 'I want no goddamn lazy schoolma'ams in my family. Balky, no good for nothing!'" After Marie got her certificate, though, he bragged about it when she wasn't around. "'That's what comes of living with an educated man!' And none denied it."[27] Clearly, Jules was willing to take credit where none was due, but it was Marie's fortitude and determination that allowed her to successfully pass the examination for which she had so little formal preparation.

Marie shows a streak of this independence from a very young age, when she plays by herself, farms the second Sandoz homestead, and even in her smart-aleck replies to her mother that risked physical retribution. When she discovered, by observation, that her mother was pregnant again, she said, "I should think you'd be tired having babies—I'm tired watching them."[28] She was not afraid to share her opinion or take the slap for doing so. Marie demonstrates an independent streak and autonomy and shows how these androgynous characteristics of independence yield successes. Further, she is able to exert agency against her mother and any others who try to enact injustices against the Sandoz family, balancing feminine and masculine traits.

Marie serves as an example of how perseverance, conviction, and intellectualism can enable success and the ability to ultimately question the social structure, characteristics that find her way into her written works. In her novel *Capital City*, the character Abigail Allerton also maintains a balance of androgynous characteristics. Allerton, an intellectual and a history professor at the Franklin University, writes an exposé novel, *Anteroom for Kingmakers*, revealing the dark world of government corruption in back-alley politics and at Franklin. In *Capital City*, the protagonist Sandoz creates aligns with the author's own activism. Abigail, the intellectual and writer, successfully exposes the ills of her corrupt society. Sandoz, too, attempts to expose injustice by publishing her book amid the concerns about society and government that were felt by many at that time. Sandoz utilizes the character of Abigail to fight for workers' equality and government accountability. In doing so she demonstrates the ills that have befallen her community as well, serving as a vehicle to reflect how government corruption pervades society. Sandoz herself "spoke of two of her characters as representing not two people, but two aspects of the artist in decaying society."[29] As a woman literary artist, Sandoz sought to show others the reality of a decaying society with metaphor, but also in truthful and factual ways.

In the novel, Abigail is able to effect change. The evolving government and some of the potential electorate and candidates maintain fascist ideas and attempt to stomp out any form of equality for the working class. Yet Abigail and others attempt to create equality and are instrumental in promoting workers' strikes across the state and in forming and encouraging cooperatives that combat the emerging fascist, reactionary government. The construction of the character, Abigail, allows Sandoz two characters to fight her own fight within the context of a novel, showing that strong women can, in fact, combat injustices that exist in society. Women are responsible for righting injustices of equality, but, at the same time, neither Sandoz nor her protagonist offer any solution or elevate one form of government over another.

It is notable that Sandoz sets her novel in a social and cultural environment that believed that women needed protection: "Women shouldn't be allowed to drink, they told each other, or to see such things as the parade today. They ought to be protected, for they were never really civilized, always hankering for the brute male no matter what their cultural background, training, or intellect."[30] As a consequence of this common positioning of women and of Abigail's attitude toward the government, her work was immediately rejected as a wasted women's tome. Yet Abigail found supporters in the community that wanted her to speak out, and some in communities outside of the corrupt Franklin City who reveled in the novel's honesty. At the end of the book, Sandoz depicts Abigail receiving a telegram from Goldwyn confirming their purchase of her book.[31]

Abigail serves as a model for how women can successfully effect change through strong convictions, intellectualism, and agency.[32]

These same characteristics of strong women are found in Sandoz's novel about a female frontier doctor who fluidly transgresses gender boundaries. In *Miss Morissa*, the protagonist, Morissa, provides Sandoz the opportunity to examine the role of womanhood in the late 1800s and early 1900s, as well as societal changes in the status of women up to her present day in 1955. Sandoz's stakes are larger than the individual; she is concerned with bringing to her readers' attention an understanding of the social position of women in their historic context, as well as the way women fit into shaping a community of equal rights activists.

This work's historical significance lies in its representation of plains women as more than submissive helpmates in the West. Indeed, Morissa presents an opposite picture of these stereotypes. The character in this novel is strong, speaks her mind, cares for her own well-being single-handedly, and attempts to grow her own identity without relying upon anyone else. Here Sandoz suggests through the protagonist that women are capable of more than unquestioningly following men. Sandoz shows how women could and did do the work of men; Morissa and the women she represents exhibit agency and ambition. As Sandoz describes her title character: "This girl who had pulled herself up from her days as a woods colt on a poor-farm was no dove or even a grouse, no matter what the wounding."[33] It is when Morissa maintains a balance of traits, a seemingly androgynous personality, that she is most successful. It is only when she wavers to one side of overpowering strength, a trait associated with masculinity, or weaker acquiescence, a trait associated with femininity, that problems arise.

Sandoz lays out the case for androgynous behavior immediately in *Miss Morissa*. The novel begins with Morissa's arrival in western Nebraska after her relationship to her fiancé, Allston Hoyt, ends. The plains challenge this proper, eastern-schooled woman, stylishly attired in a green riding habit and having been properly

JILLIAN L. WENBURG

trained in both medicine and domestic chores. Yet, Morissa meets her challenges with aplomb—diving onto a borrowed horse within the first pages of the novel to save a drowning miner. She evidences strength, fortitude, and brazenness, acting assertively in what her fellow community members might term a masculine nature; yet, she confounds them by appearing feminine in her dress and manner. She challenges the public's perception and stereotypes of women, but not to a state of alienation. Sandoz presents a balance of femininity and masculinity in her protagonist, which allows Morissa to thrive in the harsh plains environment.

Throughout the novel, Sandoz creates situations in which Morissa is pushed to succeed, challenging or surpassing women's expected roles. When the lady doctor was needed and the only horse available was not "woman-broke," the man who came to get her said, "You better get into some a Robin's work pants, and I fetched you a pair of chaps to hold off the rain, 'n spurs. This ain't the night for no lady sidesaddlin."[34] Without hesitating, Morissa donned male attire and rode astride. Without the riding skills, or the self-confidence to develop them, she would not have been able to save her patient. She also demonstrates masculine characteristics of assertion, taking charge, and assuming control when threatened on the plains by male figures, rather than looking for men to protect her. She defends herself and a wounded patient against an intruder trying to attack a home where she was helping an injured man: "With the butcher knife she dug gun slits through the sod near each corner," combining the male characteristics of protection with female attributes of care giving.[35]

Throughout the story, Morissa balances her female and male traits and, in doing so, becomes a character that echoes Sandoz's earlier characters of the balanced Marie or intellectual Abigail, doppelgangers of herself. Rather than rely upon men to support and her fulfill her, Sandoz and her characters seek a balance of male and female characteristics. In *Miss Morissa*, the protagonist presents a representation of both female and male characters that provides an alternative gendered ideal. In the novel, at the same time that Morissa engages in activities typically assigned to men, some men undertake activities that are often perceived as more feminine in nature, like cooking or caretaking. Sandoz demonstrates how the gender of the character doing the action is not important; what was more significant was the intent of the party doing the action.

It is when Morissa leans too heavily toward either femininity or masculinity, and loses the androgynous balance, that trouble befalls her. This becomes clear with the romantic relationship that develops with the character Eddie, when Morissa accesses her femininity too much, marrying Eddie. Her decision ultimately leads to the disapproval of the townspeople, who neither respect nor understand her decision. They are critical of Morissa's whimsical decision to marry and begin to shun her in public. On the other hand, when Morissa's behavior is considered too masculine, she is threatened by the local cattlemen, who view her infringement on what they consider their land with anger and resentment. Sandoz uses Morissa's character to show that androgyny, a successful balance of masculine and feminine traits, allows women to achieve the most success and reward.

The danger of an androgyny that leans too far in the masculine direction is found in Sandoz's character Gulla Slogum. In the novel *Slogum House*, Gulla displays some of the intellectual skills and abilities that Sandoz features elsewhere in her fiction. Gulla has an unfettered desire for land, which she acquires through power. She begins a takeover of the region in ingenious yet always devious ways, utilizing prostitution, fraud, and intimidation. Placed in historical context, Sandoz uses Gulla as a counterpart to worries about the Nazi regime. Just like Hitler, Gulla sought power and land with no fear of consequences. Gulla's relentless desire for land acquisition is based on traits associated with masculinity: greed, desire for more power, for autonomy, and the chance at running an autocracy. As Sandoz described Gulla in a letter, "She prostituted such beauty as fell into her hands, and destroyed the most promising individuals of the opposition. That's good dictator practice."[36] She wanted con-

JILLIAN L. WENBURG

trol and to be head of her frontier feudal territory. Sandoz's Gulla served just as she'd hoped, as "a study of a will-to-power individual and the development of the techniques of fascism" so that others could learn how these individuals rise to power and control their environments.[37] Her roles and positions on the plains indicate that Gulla used any means to make herself an independent woman. She did not rely on any outsider for work on the farm, even going so far as to employ her twin daughters as prostitutes in the brothel on the second floor of Slogum House.

Gulla's independence shows what extremes will do to a person in power, what extremes they will take to keep power. Throughout the text, Gulla's character serves as a mediator of power as she manipulated and controlled the local sheriff, the townspeople, and her own family. For example, when she felt her family was overstepping their roles, she notes, "Yes, it was time she corralled the Slogums once more."[38] Sandoz showcases Gulla's assertiveness through her emasculating treatment of her husband. This woman, whose masculine traits Sandoz has physically highlighted by portraying her with a "line of healthy down on her lip," is complicit in the castration of one of her daughter's boyfriends, of switching dead bodies that were state evidence, and other reprehensible actions that defy feminine behaviors.[39] Gulla serves as a warning character for the effect a unilateral focus has upon a person. Clearly, Gulla's one-track mind has forced her daughters into prostitution without any thoughts of the consequences, including venereal disease and forced abortions, one son sick, the other dead.[40] Gulla's character does effect change, but not in a positive way. In constructing Gulla, Sandoz suggests how great success is indeed possible on the plains, but that one must be careful in how one pursues that success. Sandoz seems to agitate here for female empowerment, though wise and balanced female empowerment.

Gulla's character might also effect change because she shows how to manipulate gender biases for her own needs. Gulla's prostitute daughters are able to exert some influence when they later rebel against their mother. Gulla utilizes the masculine system for her own benefit—to gain more acreage—and although her methods and actions are generally illegal and morally wrong, she does show that a woman can seek empowerment on the plains and be master of her own domain. However, without a balance of force, self-destruction is inevitable.

When *Slogum House* appeared in print, an *Omaha World Herald* book reviewer astutely judged Sandoz: "[The book] stamps Mari Sandoz not as a biographer of her father alone, not as one-book writer, but as one with something definite to say and the power to say it with force and clarity and sweep."[41] Sandoz's stakes for writing include not only pointing out the fallibility of the current system for women, but also attempting to provide women with a method by which to succeed. Moreover, she demonstrates how men can support women in this endeavor, thus leading to an overall stronger society. Her work comments on the fact that women were lumped into one essentialist group in the United States. Sandoz uses the past as a way to show women of the present day how they, too, can be empowered, independent, and ultimately influence future generations. Men and women all begin to work together to achieve a better frontier community and fulfill their roles. Similarly, in *Capital City* and *Slogum House*, it is through the unification of the men and women intellectuals and townspeople that they are able to achieve successes. Sandoz articulates how an imbalance of power or strict adherence to gender roles only serves to hinder a community, whether that power is based on class, race, or gender.

Throughout her works, Sandoz maintained an ability to interweave historians' realism with the storytelling of a romantic. She produced works that engage and cleave to readers' collective consciousness and changed attitudes about past female representation and writers of her time. Her writing demonstrates that androgynous characteristics play a key role in keeping society in balance as well as for fighting against injustice and in advocating for future equal rights.

JILLIAN L. WENBURG

1. Edward Weeks, *October 1935 Book-of-the-Month Club News.* Quoted in Stauffer, *Story Catcher of the Plains,* 98.
2. Yvonne Umland Smith to Helen Winter Stauffer, September 26, 1976. Quoted in Stauffer, *Story Catcher of the Plains,* 98.
3. Mari Sandoz used her literary characters to serve as social change agents. She first molded her characters in an androgynous fashion, showing how women that did not fit the traditional mold of being apologetic and meek could achieve success. She used traits such as hardiness and dirtiness as a way to achieve empowerment. She also showed how women could take this advice too far and become overly bold and ruthless. Sandoz's characters reflect how a balance of certain characteristics can lead to success for the individual and the community.
4. While Luce Irigaray later postulated in *The Sex Which is Not One* that women were not a sex, but rather, a "female imaginary" (28), Sandoz, in the early 1930s, contended—through her manipulation of the characters she wrote about—that women should not have an inscribed sex.
5. Butler, *Gender Trouble,* 3.
6. "Miss Sandoz's Big Political Cartoon," unknown, Mari Sandoz Collection (MS 080), Archives and Special Collections, University of Nebraska–Lincoln Libraries.
7. Sandoz's life and the women in her works demonstrate that she valued such androgynous attributes as a strong identity, integrity, convictions, intellectualism, independence, perseverance, and agency. Sandoz's historical fiction and personal history evidence her belief that a strong woman maintained androgynous characteristics, aiding them in rectifying injustice and inequality. She considered that certain attributes of masculinity and femininity required equilibration in order to keep society in balance and from tipping into corruption and injustice.
8. Myres, *Westering Women and the Frontier Experience,* 239.
9. Sandoz's presentation of a female utopian vision could be viewed as an opportunity to advocate for feminist rights and for solely improving the lot of females. Yet it is clear through her work and the way in which females and males interact that she is not looking solely to improve the situation for females in her society, but also to improve the relationship between all, regardless of gender.

10. Mari Sandoz to Mrs. J. W. Babcock, January 21, 1936, Mari Sandoz Collection (MS 080), Archives and Special Collections, University of Nebraska–Lincoln Libraries.

11. Mari Sandoz to Estelle Laughlin, March 27, 1940, Mari Sandoz Collection (MS 080), Archives and Special Collections, University of Nebraska–Lincoln Libraries.

12. Men and women were so involved in proving the other wrong, they were preventing one another from achieving more together on a higher plane. Her empowered female characters embody the role models that Sandoz sees thriving in an ideal societal construct: people who are strong, forceful, opinionated, and enterprising. These women do not claim to be feminist activists. She advanced a humanist agenda.

13. Sandoz, *Old Jules*, 219.

14. Sandoz, *Old Jules*, 204–5.

15. Sandoz, *Old Jules*, 196.

16. Sandoz, *Old Jules*, 248.

17. Sandoz, *Old Jules*, 183.

18. Sandoz, *Old Jules*, 198.

19. Sandoz, *Old Jules*, 222.

20. Sandoz, *Old Jules*, 216.

21. Sandoz, *Old Jules*, 230.

22. Sandoz, *Old Jules*, 284.

23. Sandoz, *Old Jules*, 296.

24. Sandoz, *Old Jules*, 293.

25. Sandoz, *Old Jules*, 294.

26. Sandoz, *Old Jules*, 340.

27. Sandoz, *Old Jules*, 366.

28. Sandoz, *Old Jules*, 341.

29. Quoted in Stauffer, *Story Catcher of the Plains*, 129.

30. Sandoz, *Capital City*, 58.

31. Sandoz, *Capital City*, 327.

32. Sandoz, *Capital City*, 327.

33. Sandoz, *Miss Morissa*, 13.

34. Sandoz, *Miss Morissa*, 47.

35. Sandoz, *Miss Morissa*, 106.

36. Mari Sandoz to P. S. Heaton, June 26, 1940, Mari Sandoz Collection (MS 080), Archives and Special Collections, University of Nebraska–Lincoln Libraries.

37. Mari Sandoz to Alfred R. McIntyre, June 15, 1944, Mari Sandoz Collection (MS 080), Archives and Special Collections, University of Nebraska–Lincoln Libraries.
38. Sandoz, *Slogum House*, 103.
39. Sandoz, *Slogum House*, 36.
40. Sandoz, *Slogum House*, 228, 66.
41. "Among the New Books: Brutal Novel: *Slogum House*," *Omaha World Herald*, November 28, 1937.

Bibliography

ARCHIVES

Mari Sandoz Collection. Archives and Special Collections. University of Nebraska–Lincoln Libraries, Lincoln, Nebraska.

McLean County Historical Society. Bloomington, Illinois.

PUBLISHED WORKS

Albers, Patricia. "New Perspectives on Plains Indian Women." In *The Hidden Half: Studies of Plains Indian Women,* edited by Patricia Albers and Beatrice Medicine, 1–26. Lanham MD: University Press of America, 1983.

Albers, Patricia, and Beatrice Medicine, eds. *The Hidden Half: Studies of Plains Indian Women.* Lanham MD: University Press of America, 1983.

Armitage, Susan H. "Western Women: Beginning to Come into Focus." *Montana, the Magazine of Western History* 32 (Summer 1982): 2–9.

Axtell, James. "Ethnohistory: An Historian's Viewpoint." *Ethnohistory* 26, no.1 (Winter 1979): 1–13.

———. "The Ethnohistory of Early America: A Review Essay." *William and Mary Quarterly,* 3rd ser., 35, no. 1 (January 1978): 110–44.

———. "The Ethnohistory of Native America." In *Rethinking American Indian History,* edited by Donald L Fixico, 11–28. Albuquerque: University of New Mexico Press, 1997.

Bailey, Beth L. "Scientific Truth . . . and Love: The Marriage Education Movement in the United States." *Journal of Social History* 20 (Summer 1987): 711–32.

Basch, Norma. "Invisible Women: The Legal Fiction of Marital Unity in Nineteenth-Century America." *Feminist Studies* 5, no. 2 (Summer 1979): 346–66.

Beasley, Maureen. *Eleanor Roosevelt and the Media: A Public Quest for Self-Fulfillment.* Urbana: University of Illinois Press, 1987.

Bergman, Andrew. *We're in the Money: Depression America and Its Films.* Chicago: Ivan R. Dee, 1993.

Berkhofer, Robert F. Jr. "Cultural Pluralism versus Ethnocentrism." In *The American Indian and the Problem of History,* edited by Calvin Martin, 35–45. New York: Oxford University Press, 1987.

Blackwelder, Julia Kirk. "Women in the Work Force: Atlanta, New Orleans, and San Antonio, 1930 to 1940." *Journal of Urban History* 4 (May 1978): 331–53.

———. *Women of the Depression: Caste and Culture in San Antonio, 1929–1939.* College Station: Texas A&M University Press, 1984.

Boas, Franz. *A Franz Boas Reader: The Shaping of American Anthropology: 1883–1911.* Edited by George W. Stocking Jr. Chicago: University of Chicago Press, 1989.

Boris, Eileen. "Regulating Industrial Homework: The Triumph of "Sacred Motherhood." *Journal of American History* 71 (March 1985): 745–63.

Butler, Anne M. *Daughters of Joy, Sisters of Misery.* Urbana: University of Illinois Press, 1985.

———. "Military Myopia: Prostitution on the Frontier." *Prologue* 13 (Winter 1981): 233–50.

Butler, Judith. *Gender Trouble: Feminism and the Subversion of Identity.* New York: Routledge, 1990.

Brown, Dee. *The Gentle Tamers: Women of the Old Wild West.* Lincoln: University of Nebraska Press, 1958.

Castaneda, Antonia I. "Women of Color and the Rewriting of Western History: The Discourse, Politics, and Decolonization of History." *Pacific Historical Review* 61 (November 1992): 501–34.

Caughfield, Adrienne. *True Women and the Western Experience.* College Station: Texas A&M University Press, 2005.

Checkoway, Julie. "Mail-Order Brides." In *Encyclopedia of the Great Plains,* edited by David Wishart, 332. Lincoln: University of Nebraska Press, 2004.

Chused, Richard H. "Late Nineteenth Century Married Women's Property Law: Reception of the Early Married Women's Property Acts by Courts and Legislatures." *American Journal of Legal History* 29, no. 1 (January 1985): 3–35.

———. "The Oregon Donation Act of 1850 and Nineteenth-Century Federal Married Women's Property Law." *Law and History Review* 2, no. 1 (Spring 1984): 44–78.

Cook, Blanche Weisen. *Eleanor Roosevelt, 1844–1933.* New York: Viking Press, 1992.

Cook-Lynn, Elizabeth. *Anti-Indianism in Modern America: A Voice from Tatekeya's Earth.* Urbana and Chicago: University of Illinois Press, 2001.

Cott, Nancy F. *The Grounding of Modern Feminism.* New Haven: Yale University Press, 1987.

Cronon, William, George Miles, and Jay Gitlin. "Becoming West: Toward a New Meaning for Western History." In *Under an Open Sky: Rethinking America's Western Past,* edited by William Cronon, George Miles, and Jay Gitlin, 3–27. New York: W.W. Norton, 1992.

Dick, Everett. *The Sod-House Frontier 1845–1890.* New York: Appleton-Century, 1937.

———. "Sunbonnet and Calico, The Homesteader's Consort." *Nebraska History* 47 (March 1966): 3–13.

Diffendal, Anne P. "Prostitution in Grand Island, Nebraska, 1870–1913." *Heritage of the Great Plains* 16 (Summer 1983): 1–10.

Downey, Betsy. "Battered Pioneers: Jules Sandoz and the Physical Abuse of Wives on the American Frontier." *Great Plains Quarterly* 12 (Winter 1992): 31–49.

———. "She Does Not Write like a Historian: Mari Sandoz and the Old and New Western History." *Great Plains Quarterly* 16 (Winter 1996): 9–28.

Duron, Clementina. "Mexican Women and Labor Conflict in Los Angeles: The ILGWU Dressmakers' Strike of 1933." *Aztlan* 15 (Spring 1984): 365–75.

Edmunds, R. David. "Native Americans, New Voices: American Indian History, 1895–1995." *American Historical Review* 100, no. 3 (June 1995): 717–40.

Edson, John Thomas. *Wanted: Belle Starr.* London: Severn House, 1983.

Faragher, John Mack. *Women and Men on the Overland Trail.* New Haven: Yale University Press, 2001.

Fixico, Donald Lee. *Termination and Relocation: Federal Indian Policy, 1945–1960.* Albuquerque: University of New Mexico Press, 1986.

Ford, Ramona. "Native American Women: Changing Statuses, Changing Interpretations." In *Writing the Range: Race, Class and Culture in the Women's West,* edited by Elizabeth Jameson and Susan Armitage, 42–68. Norman: University of Oklahoma Press, 1997.

Friedan, Betty. *The Feminist Mystique.* New York: W.W. Norton, 1963.

Garland, Hamlin. *A Pioneer Mother.* Chicago: Bookfellows, 1922.

Gonda, Susan. "Not a Matter of Choice: San Diego Women and Divorce 1850–1880." *Journal of San Diego History* 37 (Summer 1991): 194–213.

Goss, Kristin A. *The Paradox of Gender Equality: How American Women's Groups Gained and Lost Their Public Vote.* Ann Arbor: University of Michigan Press, 2013.

Graulich, Melody. "Every Husband's Right: Sex Roles in Mari Sandoz's *Old Jules.*" *Western American Literature* (May 1983): 14–20.

———. "Violence Against Women in Literature of the Western Family." *Frontiers* 7 (Summer 1984): 14–20.

Green, Carl R. *Belle Starr.* Hillside NJ: Enslow Publishers, 1992.

Greenwell, Scott L. "Fascists in Fiction: Two Early Novels of Mari Sandoz." *Western American Literature* 12 (1977): 133–43.

Griswold del Castillo, Richard. *La Familia: Chicano Families in the Urban Southwest, 1848 to the Present.* Notre Dame: University of Notre Dame Press, 1984.

Griswold, Robert L. "Apart but Not Adrift: Wives, Divorce, and Independence in California, 1850–1890." *Pacific Historical Review* 49 (May 1980): 265–84.

———. *Family and Divorce in California, 1850–1890.* Albany: State University of New York Press, 1982.

Hardcastle, Stoney. *The Legend of Belle Starr.* New York: Carlyle Communications, 1979.

Hicks, Edwin P. *Belle Starr and Her Pearl.* Little Rock: C.A. Harper, 1963.

Hirata, Lucie Cheng. "Free, Indentured, Enslaved: Chinese Prostitutes in 19th-Century America." *Signs* 5 (Autumn 1979): 3–29.

Honey, Maureen. "Images of Women in *The Saturday Evening Post, 1931–36.*" *Journal of Popular Culture* 10 (Fall 1976): 352–58.

Hough, Emerson. *The Passing of the Frontier.* New Haven: Yale University Press, 1921.

Irigaray, Luce. *This Sex Which Is Not One.* Translated by Catherine Porter with Carolyn Burke. Ithaca: Cornell University Press, 1985.

Jackson, Brenda K. *Domesticating the West: The Re-Creation of the Nineteenth-Century Middle Class.* Lincoln: University of Nebraska Press, 2005.

Jameson, Elizabeth. "Women as Workers, Women as Civilizers: True Womanhood in the American West." *Frontiers* 7 (1984): 1–8.

——— and Susan Armitage. Editors' introduction to *Writing the Range: Race, Class, and Culture in the Women's West,* edited by Elizabeth Jameson and Susan Armitage, 3–16. Norman: University of Oklahoma Press, 1997.

Jameson, Fredric. *Archaeologies of the Future: The Desire Called Utopia and Other Science Fictions.* London: Verso, 2007.

Jensen, Joan M. "The Death of Rosa: Sexuality in Rural America." *Agricultural History* 67 (Fall 1993): 1–12.

Jenson, Joan M., and Darlis Miller. "The Gentle Tamers Revisited: New Approaches to the History of Women in the American West." *Pacific Historical Review* 69 (May 1980): 173–213.

Johannsen, Robert. "The Meaning of Manifest Destiny." In *Manifest Destiny and Empire: American Antebellum Expansion*, edited by Sam W. Haynes and Christopher Morris, 7–20. Arlington: University of Texas Press, 1997.

Johnson, Maurice. "The Prairie Schooner: Ten Years." *Prairie Schooner* 11, no. 1 (Spring 1937): 71–82.

Johnson, Nancy B. "Mad Pioneer Women." In *Encyclopedia of the Great Plains*, edited by David Wishart, 392. Lincoln: University of Nebraska Press, 2004.

Kaplin, Amy. "Manifest Domesticity." *American Literature* (September 1998): 581–606.

Knights of Ak-Sar-Ben. "Building a Prosperous Heartland since 1895." Knights of Ak-Sar-Ben Foundation Website–History. Accessed November 3, 2011. https://www.aksarben.org/p/about/knightsofaksarben.

Larson, T. A. "Dolls, Vassals, and Drudges—Pioneer Women in the West." *Western Historical Quarterly* 3 (January 1972): 5–16.

———. "Women's Role in the American West." *Montana, the Magazine of Western History* 24 (Summer 1974): 2–11.

Laughlin, Estelle Chrisman. "Dr. Georgia Arbuckle Fix: Pioneer." In *Pioneer Tales of the North Platte Valley and Nebraska Panhandle*, edited by A. B. Wood, 21–39. Gering NE: Courier Press, 1938.

Lichty, Kathryne L. "A History of the Settlement of the Nebraska Sandhills, 1912–1990." Master's thesis, University of Wyoming, 1960.

Limbaugh, Elaine E. "A Feminist Reads *Old Jules*." *Platte Valley Review* 17 (Winter 1989): 41–50.

Limerick, Patricia Nelson. *The Legacy of Conquest: The Unbroken Past of the American West*. New York: W.W. Norton, 1988.

Lindgren, H. Elaine. *Land in her Own Name: Women as Homesteaders in North Dakota*. Norman: University of Oklahoma Press, 1996.

Matthiessen, Peter. *In the Spirit of Crazy Horse*. New York: Viking, 1983. Reprint, New York: Penguin, 1991.

Mason, Katherine A. "Greed and the Erosion of the Pioneer Ethic: Selected Novels of Mari Sandoz." *Platte Valley Review* 17 (Winter 1989): 92–101.

Mattern, Claire. "Mari Sandoz: Her Use of Allegory in *Slogum House*." PhD diss., University of Nebraska–Lincoln, 1981.

———. "Rebels, Aliens, Outsiders, and the Nonconformist in the Writings of Mari Sandoz." *CEA Critic* 49 (Winter/Summer 1986–87): 102–13.

McCormick, John S. "Red Lights in Zion: Salt Lake City's Stockade, 1908–11." *Utah Historical Quarterly* 50, no. 2 (Spring 1982): 168–81.

Mencken, H. L. *The Philosophy of Friedrich Nietzsche.* Port Washington NY: Kennikat Press, 1968.

Murphy, Mary. "The Private Lives of Public Women: Prostitution in Butte, Montana, 1878–1917." *Frontiers* 7 (Fall 1984): 30–35.

Myres, Sandra L. *Westering Women and the Frontier Experience 1800–1915.* Albuquerque: University of New Mexico Press, 1982.

Nietzsche, Friedrich. The Will to Power. Edited by Oscar Levy. Translated by Anthony M. Ludovici. Vol. 15 of The Complete Works of Friedrich Nietzsche. London: George Allen and Unwin, 1924.

Oshana, Maryann. "Native American Women in Westerns: Reality and Myth." *Frontiers* 6 (Fall 1981): 46–50.

Ostenso, Martha. *O River Remember.* New York: Dodd, Mead, 1943.

———. *Wild Geese.* New York: Dodd, Mead, 1925.

Patterson-Black, Sheryll. "Women Homesteaders on the Great Plains Frontier." *Frontiers* 1, no. 2 (Spring 1976): 67–88.

Patterson, James I. "Mary Dewson and the American Minimum Wage Movement." *Labor History* 5 (Spring 1964): 134–52.

Petrik, Paula. "If She Be Content: The Development of Montana Divorce Law, 1865–1907." *Western Historical Quarterly* 18 (July 1987): 261–92.

———. "Prostitution in Helena, Montana, 1865–1900." *Montana: The Magazine of Western History* 35 (Summer 1985): 2–13.

Pifer, Caroline Sandoz, and Jules Sandoz Jr. *Son of Old Jules: Memoirs of Jules Sandoz, Jr.* Lincoln: University of Nebraska Press, 1962.

Pound, Louise. "Nebraska Rain Lore and Rain Making." *California Folklore Quarterly* 5, no. 2 (April 1946): 129–42.

Powell, Father Peter J. "Bearer of Beauty: Woman of the Sand Hills." *Platte Valley Review* 17, no. 1 (Winter 1989): 3–16.

Radke-Moss, Andrea G. "'Willing Challengers': Women's Experiences on the Northern Plains, 1862–1930." In *Women on the North American Plains,* edited by Renee M. Laegreid and Sandra Mathews, 48–67. Lubbock: Texas Tech University Press, 2011.

Riley, Glenda. *Building and Breaking Families in the American West.* Albuquerque: University of New Mexico Press, 1996.

———. "Continuity and Change: Interpreting Women in Western History." *Journal of the West* 32 (July 1993): 7–11.

———. *Divorce: An American Tradition.* New York: Oxford University Press, 1991.

————. *The Female Frontier: A Comparative View of Women on the Prairies and the Plains*. Lawrence: University Press of Kansas, 1988.

————. "The Historiography of American Indian and Other Western Women." In *Rethinking American Indian History*, edited by Donald L Fixico, 43–70. Albuquerque: University of New Mexico Press, 1997.

————. "Images of the Frontierswoman: Iowa as a Case Study." *Western Historical Quarterly* 8 (April 1977): 189–202.

————. *Inventing the American Woman: An Inclusive History, Vol. 2: Since 1877*. Wheeling IL: Harlan Davidson, 1995.

————. "Mari Sandoz's *Slogum House*: Greed as Woman." *Great Plains Quarterly* 16 (Winter 1996): 29–41.

————. "Torn Asunder: Divorce in Early Oklahoma Territory." *Chronicles of Oklahoma* 77 (Winter 1989–90): 61–71.

Rippey, Barbara. "Mari Sandoz' Historical Perspective: Linking Past and Present." *Platte Valley Review* 17 (Winter 1989): 60–68.

Rowland, Mary C. *As Long as Life: The Memoirs of a Frontier Woman Doctor*. Seattle: Storm Peak Press, 1994.

Sandoz, Mari. *Capital City*. Boston: Little, Brown, 1939.

————. *Cheyenne Autumn*. New York: McGraw-Hill, 1953.

————. *Crazy Horse: The Strange Man of the Oglalas*. New York: Knopf, 1942. Reprint, Lincoln: University of Nebraska Press, 1992.

————. "Letter for a Seventh Birthday." *Prairie Schooner* 40, no. 4, Fortieth Anniversary Issue, (Winter 1966/67): 285–88.

————. *Letters of Mari Sandoz*. Edited by Helen Winter Stauffer. Lincoln: University of Nebraska Press, 1992.

————. *Miss Morissa: Doctor of the Gold Trail*. New York: McGraw-Hill, 1955. Reprint, Lincoln: University of Nebraska Press, 1980.

————. *Old Jules*. Boston: Little, Brown, 1935. Reprint, Lincoln: University of Nebraska Press, 1985.

————. *Old Jules Country*. New York: Hastings House, 1965.

————. *Slogum House*. New York: Little, Brown, 1937. Reprint, Lincoln: University of Nebraska Press, 1981.

————. "The Stranger at the Curb." *Mid-American Review of Sociology* 13 (Winter 1988): 31–42.

————. *These Were the Sioux*. Lincoln: University of Nebraska Press, 1961. Reprint, Lincoln: University of Nebraska Press, 1985.

―――. "The Vine." In *Hostiles and Friendlies: Short Writings of Mari Sandoz*, 117–125. Lincoln: University of Nebraska Press, 1992.

―――. "What I Learned from the Indians." *Denver Post Empire Magazine*, February 24, 1952, 8–9.

―――. "What the Sioux Taught Me." *Reader's Digest* (May 1952): 121–24.

Scharf, Lois. *Eleanor Roosevelt: The First Lady of American Liberalism*. Boston: G. K. Hall, 1987.

―――. *To Work and to Wed: Female Employment, Feminism, and the Great Depression*. Westport CT: Greenwood Press, 1980.

Schlissel, Lillian. "Frontier Families: Crises in Ideology." In *The American Self: Myth, Ideology, and Popular Culture*, edited by Sam B. Girgus, 155–65. Albuquerque: University of New Mexico Press, 1981.

Schwieder, Dorothy, and Deborah Fink. "Plains Women: Rural Life in the 1930s." *Great Plains Quarterly* 8 (Spring 1988): 79–88.

Shirley, Betty M. *Belle Starr and Her Roots*. Cupertino CA: Shirley Association, 1989.

Shirley, Glenn. *Belle Starr and Her Times*. Norman: University of Oklahoma Press, 1982.

―――. *Outlaw Queen: The Fantastic True Story of Belle Starr*. Derby CT: Monarch, 1960.

Smith, Elaine M. "Mary McLeod Bethune." In *Black Women in America: An Historical Encyclopedia*, edited by Darlene Clark Hine, 113–27. Brooklyn: Carlson, 1993.

Sochen, June. *Mae West: She Who Laughs, Lasts*. Wheeling IL: Harlan Davidson, 1992.

―――. "Mildred Pierce and Women in Film." *American Quarterly* 30 (Spring 1978): 3–20.

Stanley, Mack. *Belle Starr's Life and Hard Times*. Spiro OK: Stanley, 1989.

Stauffer, Helen W. "Mari Sandoz." In *A Literary History of the American West*. Fort Worth: Texas Christian University Press, 1987.

―――. *Mari Sandoz*. Western Writers Series, no. 63. Boise: Boise State University Printing and Graphics Services, 1984.

―――. "Mari Sandoz and the University of Nebraska." *Prairie Schooner* 55, no. 1/2 (Spring/Summer 1981).

―――. *Mari Sandoz: Story Catcher of the Plains*. Lincoln: University of Nebraska Press, 1982.

Phillip W. Steele, *Starr Tracks: Belle and Pearl Starr*. Gretna LA: Pelican, 1989.

Stoeltje, Beverly J. "'A Helpmate for Man Indeed': The Image of the Frontier Woman." *Journal of American Folklore* 88, no. 347, Women and Folklore (January–March 1975): 25–41.

Swain, Martha H. "'The Forgotten Woman': Ellen S. Woodward and Women's Relief in the New Deal." *Prologue* 15 (Winter 1983): 200–213.

Switzer, Dorothy Nott. "Mari Sandoz's Lincoln Years: A Personal Recollection." *Prairie Schooner* 45, no 2, (Summer 1971): 107–15.

Tong, Benson. *Unsubmissive Women: Chinese Prostitutes in Nineteenth-Century San Francisco.* Norman: University of Oklahoma Press, 1994.

Underwood, June O. "Western Women and True Womanhood: Culture and Symbol in History and Literature." *Great Plains Quarterly* 5 (Spring 1985): 93–106.

Webb, Walter Prescott. *The Great Plains.* Lincoln: University of Nebraska Press, 1962.

———. *The Great Plains.* Boston: Ginn, 1931.

Wegars, Priscilla. "'Inmates of Body Houses': Prostitution in Moscow, Idaho, 1885–1910." *Idaho Yesterdays* 33 (Spring 1989): 25–37.

Weist, Katherine M. "Plains Indian Women: An Assessment." In *Anthropology on the Great Plains,* edited by W. Raymond Wood and Margot Liberty, 255–271. Lincoln: University of Nebraska Press, 1980.

Welter, Barbara. "The Cult of True Womanhood, 1820–1860." *American Quarterly* 18, no. 2 (Summer 1966): 151–74.

Westin, Jeanne. *Making Do: How Women Survived the Depression.* Chicago: Follett, 1976.

Whitaker, Rosemary. "Violence in *Old Jules* and *Slogum House.*" *Western American Literature* 16, no. 2 (November 1981): 217–24.

Winn, Robert G. *Two Starrs: Belle, the Bandit Queen, Pearl, Riverfront Madame.* Fayetteville: Washington County Historical Society, 1979.

Wortman, Roy. "Gender Issues in the National Farmers Union in the 1930s." *Midwest Review* 15 (1993): 71–83.

Youngs, J. William. *Eleanor Roosevelt: A Personal and Public Life.* Boston: Little, Brown, 1985.

Yuvajita, Phachee. "The Changing Images of Women in Western American Literature as Illustrated in the Works of Willa Cather, Hamlin Garland, and Mari Sandoz." PhD diss., University of Oregon, 1985.

Zeigler, Sara. "Uniformity and Conformity: Regionalism and the Adjudication of the Married Women's Property Acts." *Polity* 28, no. 4 (Summer 1996): 474–95.

Zunz, Olivier. *Making America Corporate, 1870-1920.* Chicago: University of Chicago Press, 1990.

Contributors

RENÉE M. LAEGREID is professor of history at the University of Wyoming. She specializes in the history of the American West, with a focus on gender and culture in the late nineteenth to mid-twentieth century. Her current research projects involve cultural and social analysis of western iconography, examining how symbols of the West have been created and shaped over time, and across international boundaries. She is the coeditor of *Women on the North American Plains* (2011), with Sandra Mathews, and author of *Riding Pretty: Rodeo Royalty in the West* (2007).

LISA POLLARD is a distance education adjunct of history at Western Wyoming Community College. She received her doctorate at the University of Nebraska–Lincoln, studying violence and LGBT activism in the modern American West as a participant of the Women's Studies Program.

GLENDA RILEY is an American historian best known for her works on women's history and women in the American West. From 1991 until her retirement in 2003, she was Alexander M. Bracken Professor of History at Ball State University. She is the author of *Women and Indians on the Frontier, 1825–1915* (1984), *The Female Frontier: A Comparative View of Women on the Prairie and the Plains* (1988), *Women and Nature: Saving the Wild West* (1999), and *The Life and Legacy of Annie Oakley* (2012). An advocate for women's history, she was inducted into the Iowa Women's Hall of Fame in 1990.

SHANNON D. SMITH is executive director for the Wyoming Humanities Council. She studied American history at the University of Nebraska–Lincoln and has written extensively on western history, American Indian history, and western women's history. Her book *Give Me Eighty Men: Women and the Myth of the Fetterman Fight* (2008) won the 2009 Wyoming State Historical Society nonfiction book award.

JILLIAN L. WENBURG, originally from southwestern Nebraska, is a lecturer for the writing program at Fort Lewis College in Durango, Colorado. Her areas of specialty include twentieth-century American literature, western literature, and the history of the American West. She received her doctorate in English and history at the University of Missouri–Kansas City, where her research centered on western author Mari Sandoz.

JOHN WUNDER is emeritus professor of history at the University of Nebraska–Lincoln. He specializes in the history of the American West, Native America, the Great Plains, colonial America, and U.S. legal history. He is the author or editor of numerous books, including *The Nebraska-Kansas Act of 1854* (2008), *Native American Sovereignty* (1999), and *Native American Cultural and Religious Freedoms* (1999). From 1988 to 1997, he was director of the Center for Great Plains Studies at Nebraska.

Index

Macumber, Wray (husband of Sandoz), 39

marriage and family: divorce, 13, 39, 78; dysfunctional, 37, 78–79, 120–21; motherhood, 3–4, 65, 74, 81–82; and property rights, 7–8; prospects on frontier, 14–17; school courses on, 74; and singlehood, 11–13; and widowhood, 13–14

masculinity, 41, 42–43, 101, 102, 122, 124–28

Mason, Katharine, 65

Mattern, Claire, 74

men. *See* gender; marriage and family

Middleton, John, 80

The Migrant Mother (Lange), 73

Miles, George, 98

Miss Morissa (Sandoz), 12, 75, 105, 124–26

morality: good *vs.* evil motif, 66–69; and good woman stereotype, 3–4, 15–17; greed as woman, 76, 82–83. *See also* bad woman stereotype

Moreno, Luisa, 72

mortality, on frontier, 13–14

motherhood, 3–4, 65, 74, 81–82

Murky River/The Ungirt Runner (Sandoz), 44

Myres, Sandra, 117

mysticism, 38

Native Americans, *87*; land claims, 87, 99–100, 104–6; Sandoz's research on, 1, 95–97, 102–3, 105–8; trends in scholarship on, 95–96, 98–102

New Women, 12

Nietzsche, Friedrich, 70

Oakley, Annie, 101

O'Brien, Edward J., 40

Old Jules (Sandoz): gender identity in, 75, 119–22; insanity in, 5, 38; literary comparisons, 78; marriage in, 14–17, 37; morality in, 6, 17–18; settlement prospects in, 10, 46–47n7; snakes in, 44–45

oral tradition, 97–98

Oregon Donation Act (1850), 9

Oregon Territory, 6, 8–9, 20n24

O River Remember (Ostenso), 77–78

Ostenso, Martha, 77–78

Owen, Ruth Bryan, 73

Patterson-Black, Sheryll, 11

Perkins, Frances, 73

physicians, female, 12–13, 75

Pike, Zebulon, 7

Plains Indians. *See* Native Americans

Polk, James K., 21n24

Pound, Louise, 38

Powers, Edward, 38

property ownership, 7–11, 99–100, 104–6

prostitution, 67, 81–82

Radke-Moss, Andrea, 10–11

Rain God Association, 38

rainmaking theories, 38

Reader's Digest, 105, 106–8

relocation and termination policy, 87, 104–6

revivals, 38

Rice, John, 43

Thorpe, J. Dayton and Abbie, 78–79
Thurston, Samuel R., 9
Turner, Frederick Jackson, 98

The Ungirt Runner/Murky River (Sandoz), 44

"The Vine" (Sandoz), 25–34; connection to classical Greek and Judeo-Christian tradition, 43–45; context of, 36–39; as East *vs.* West allegory, 40–42; publication of, 39–40; as study of masculinity, 42–43

Warren, G. K., 7
Webb, Walter Prescott, 4–5, 10, 36, 45
West: *vs.* East motif, 40–42, 69–70; mythology and stereotypes of, 2–6, 74–77; settlement in, 6–11; trends in scholarship on, 98–102
West, Mae, 73
Westering Women and the Frontier Experience 1800–1915 (Myres), 117

"What the Sioux Taught Me" (Sandoz), 89–93, 105. See also *These Were the Sioux*
White, Richard, 98–99
wicked women. *See* bad woman stereotype
widowhood, 13–14
Wild Geese (Ostenso), 78
will-to-power individual, 70, 76
The Wind (film), 4
women: during Depression, 71–74; labor divisions, 2–3, 12; property rights, 7–11; trends in scholarship on, 95–96, 98–99, 101–3. *See also* gender; marriage and family; stereotypes
women's rights movement, 118, 129n9
women's studies, 98–99, 101
Woodward, Ellen Sullivan, 72
work: during Depression, 71–73; gendered, 2–3, 12; workers' rights, 123
Woster, Donald, 98–99
Wright, Carroll D., 78

IN THE SANDOZ STUDIES SERIES

Sandoz Studies, Volume 1: Women in the Writings of Mari Sandoz
Edited and with an introduction by Renée M. Laegreid
and Shannon D. Smith
Foreword by John Wunder

To order or obtain more information on these or other University of
Nebraska Press titles, visit nebraskapress.unl.edu.